Chinese Horoscope
for 1993

About the Author

Neil Somerville is one of the leading writers in the West on Chinese horoscopes. He has been interested in Eastern forms of divination for many years and believes that much can be learned from the ancient wisdom of the East. His annual book on Chinese horoscopes has built up an international following and *Your Chinese Horoscope for 1993* marks the sixth year of publication.

Neil Somerville was born in the year of the Water Snake. His wife was born under the sign of the Monkey, his son is an Ox and baby daughter a Horse.

Your
Chinese Horoscope
for 1993

Neil Somerville

What the Year of the Rooster holds in store for you

Aquarian/Thorsons
An Imprint of HarperCollinsPublishers

The Aquarian Press
An Imprint of HarperCollins*Publishers*
77–85 Fulham Palace Road,
Hammersmith, London W6 8JB

Published by The Aquarian Press 1992
1   3   5   7   9   10   8   6   4   2

Illustrations by John Davis

A catalogue record for this book
is available from the British Library

ISBN 1 85538 171 0

Typeset by Harper Phototypesetters Limited,
Northampton, England
Printed in Great Britain by
HarperCollinsManufacturing Glasgow

Contents

Introduction   7
The Chinese Years   9
Welcome to the Year of the Rooster   13

The Rat   19
The Ox   33
The Tiger   47
The Rabbit   61
The Dragon   75
The Snake   89
The Horse   103
The Goat   117
The Monkey   131
The Rooster   145
The Dog   159
The Pig   173

Appendix: Relationships   185
         Your Ascendant   188
         How to Get the Best from the Year   190

To Ros, Richard and Emily.

Introduction

The origins of Chinese horoscopes have been lost in the mists of time. It is known that oriental astrologers practised their art many thousands of years ago and, even today, Chinese astrology continues to fascinate and intrigue.

In Chinese astrology there are 12 signs named after 12 different animals. No one quite knows how the signs acquired their names, but there is one legend that offers an explanation.

According to this legend, one Chinese New Year, the Buddha invited all the animals in his kingdom to come before him. Unfortunately – for reasons best known to the animals – only 12 turned up. The first to arrive was the Rat, followed by the Ox, Tiger, Rabbit, Dragon, Snake, Horse, Goat, Monkey, Rooster, Dog and finally the Pig.

In gratitude, the Buddha decided to name a year after each of the animals and those born during that year would inherit some of the personality of that animal. Therefore those born in the year of the Ox would be hard working, resolute and stubborn – just like the Ox; those born in the year of the Dog would be loyal and faithful – just like the Dog.

While not everyone can possibly share all the characteristics of a sign, it is incredible what similarities do occur, and this is partly where the fascination of Chinese horoscopes lies.

In addition to the 12 signs of the Chinese zodiac there are also 5 elements and these have a strengthening or moderating influence upon the sign. Details about the effects of the elements are described in each of the chapters on the 12 signs.

To find out which sign you were born under, refer to the tables on pages 9–11. As the Chinese year is based on the lunar year and does not start until late January or early February, it is particularly important for anyone born in those two months to check carefully the dates of the Chinese year in which they were born.

Also included, in the appendix, are two charts showing the compatibility between the signs for both personal and business relationships, and details about the signs ruling the different hours of the day. From this it is possible to locate your ascendant and, as in Western astrology, this has a significant influence on your personality.

In writing this book, I have taken the unusual step of combining the intriguing nature of Chinese horoscopes with the Western desire to know what the future holds, and have based my interpretations upon various factors relating to each of the signs. This is the sixth year in which *Your Chinese Horoscope* has been published and I am pleased that so many have found the sections on the forthcoming year of benefit and that the advice has been constructive and helpful. Remember, though, that at all times you are the master of your own destiny. I sincerely hope that your Chinese horoscope for 1993 will prove interesting and helpful for the year ahead.

The Chinese Years

Rat	31 January	1900	to	18 February 1901
Ox	19 February	1901	to	7 February 1902
Tiger	8 February	1902	to	28 January 1903
Rabbit	29 January	1903	to	15 February 1904
Dragon	16 February	1904	to	3 February 1905
Snake	4 February	1905	to	24 January 1906
Horse	25 January	1906	to	12 February 1907
Goat	13 February	1907	to	1 February 1908
Monkey	2 February	1908	to	21 January 1909
Rooster	22 January	1909	to	9 February 1910
Dog	10 February	1910	to	29 January 1911
Pig	30 January	1911	to	17 February 1912
Rat	18 February	1912	to	5 February 1913
Ox	6 February	1913	to	25 January 1914
Tiger	26 January	1914	to	13 February 1915
Rabbit	14 February	1915	to	2 February 1916
Dragon	3 February	1916	to	22 January 1917
Snake	23 January	1917	to	10 February 1918
Horse	11 February	1918	to	31 January 1919
Goat	1 February	1919	to	19 February 1920
Monkey	20 February	1920	to	7 February 1921
Rooster	8 February	1921	to	27 January 1922
Dog	28 January	1922	to	15 February 1923
Pig	16 February	1923	to	4 February 1924
Rat	5 February	1924	to	24 January 1925
Ox	25 January	1925	to	12 February 1926
Tiger	13 February	1926	to	1 February 1927
Rabbit	2 February	1927	to	22 January 1928
Dragon	23 January	1928	to	9 February 1929

Snake	10 February	1929	to	29 January	1930
Horse	30 January	1930	to	16 February	1931
Goat	17 February	1931	to	5 February	1932
Monkey	6 February	1932	to	25 January	1933
Rooster	26 January	1933	to	13 February	1934
Dog	14 February	1934	to	3 February	1935
Pig	4 February	1935	to	23 January	1936
Rat	24 January	1936	to	10 February	1937
Ox	11 February	1937	to	30 January	1938
Tiger	31 January	1938	to	18 February	1939
Rabbit	19 February	1939	to	7 February	1940
Dragon	8 February	1940	to	26 January	1941
Snake	27 January	1941	to	14 February	1942
Horse	15 February	1942	to	4 February	1943
Goat	5 February	1943	to	24 January	1944
Monkey	25 January	1944	to	12 February	1945
Rooster	13 February	1945	to	1 February	1946
Dog	2 February	1946	to	21 January	1947
Pig	22 January	1947	to	9 February	1948
Rat	10 February	1948	to	28 January	1949
Ox	29 January	1949	to	16 February	1950
Tiger	17 February	1950	to	5 February	1951
Rabbit	6 February	1951	to	26 January	1952
Dragon	27 January	1952	to	13 February	1953
Snake	14 February	1953	to	2 February	1954
Horse	3 February	1954	to	23 January	1955
Goat	24 January	1955	to	11 February	1956
Monkey	12 February	1956	to	30 January	1957
Rooster	31 January	1957	to	17 February	1958
Dog	18 February	1958	to	7 February	1959
Pig	8 February	1959	to	27 January	1960
Rat	28 January	1960	to	14 February	1961
Ox	15 February	1961	to	4 February	1962
Tiger	5 February	1962	to	24 January	1963
Rabbit	25 January	1963	to	12 February	1964
Dragon	13 February	1964	to	1 February	1965
Snake	2 February	1965	to	20 January	1966

Horse	21 January	1966	to	8 February	1967
Goat	9 February	1967	to	29 January	1968
Monkey	30 January	1968	to	16 February	1969
Rooster	17 February	1969	to	5 February	1970
Dog	6 February	1970	to	26 January	1971
Pig	27 January	1971	to	14 February	1972
Rat	15 February	1972	to	2 February	1973
Ox	3 February	1973	to	22 January	1974
Tiger	23 January	1974	to	10 February	1975
Rabbit	11 February	1975	to	30 January	1976
Dragon	31 January	1976	to	17 February	1977
Snake	18 February	1977	to	6 February	1978
Horse	7 February	1978	to	27 January	1979
Goat	28 January	1979	to	15 February	1980
Monkey	16 February	1980	to	4 February	1981
Rooster	5 February	1981	to	24 January	1982
Dog	25 January	1982	to	12 February	1983
Pig	13 February	1983	to	1 February	1984
Rat	2 February	1984	to	19 February	1985
Ox	20 February	1985	to	8 February	1986
Tiger	9 February	1986	to	28 January	1987
Rabbit	29 January	1987	to	16 February	1988
Dragon	17 February	1988	to	5 February	1989
Snake	6 February	1989	to	26 January	1990
Horse	27 January	1990	to	14 February	1991
Goat	15 February	1991	to	3 February	1992
Monkey	4 February	1992	to	22 January	1993
Rooster	23 January	1993	to	9 February	1994

Note: The names of the signs in the Chinese zodiac occasionally differ in the various books on Chinese astrology, although the characteristics of that sign remains the same. In some books the Ox is referred to as the Buffalo or Bull, the Rabbit as the Hare or Cat, the Goat as the Sheep and the Pig as the Boar.

For the sake of convenience, the male gender is used throughout this book. Unless otherwise stated, the characteristics of the signs apply to both sexes.

Fortune turns like a wheel.

Chinese proverb.

Welcome to the Year of the Rooster

The Rooster is a busy bird. From his shrill, early morning 'Cock-a-doodle-do' to sundown, he is continually active. Proudly and majestically strutting around many a farmyard, the Rooster likes to survey all that is going on, his beady, penetrating eyes continually alert.

The Rooster is distinctive in appearance and appears methodical, efficient and active. This desire for action and for practical efficiency will help to set the tone for 1993, the year of the Rooster. The Chinese New Year begins on 23 January 1993 and this will be a year of optimism and considerable potential. For those who act positively and determinedly, the rewards can be great. Tradition has it that the Rooster year is a year of achievement, when hard work, discipline and attention to detail will bring success.

Previous Rooster years have indeed witnessed many historic and major achievements, which were often the culmination of many years of preparation. It was in 1969, a Rooster year, when man made that historic first step on the moon and 60 years earlier when Henry Ford totally transformed the motor industry by introducing the 'assembly line' method of production. Rooster years are years of dedication, years for putting practical ideas into action. For those sufficiently motivated, 1993 can be a most important year.

There will be a general improvement in the economies of many countries around the world in 1993 and many industries will finally pull out of a recession which has dogged their progress in recent years. Engineering, technology, consumer-related industries and the catering industry in particular are likely to do well. The Rooster year will also be quite an active year politically. Groups and nationalities that have been suppressed or subjected to injustices in the past will be active in making their plight heard. Likewise, those with grievances and campaigners for certain causes will succeed in attracting the attention of those in authority. Previous Rooster years have been marked by many large and significant campaigns and 1993 will be no exception. It was in 1969 when millions of Americans demonstrated against the Vietnam war and 12 years later when Britain witnessed the large-scale 'People's March for Jobs', while in Amsterdam 400,000 demonstrated against nuclear missiles. Similar large protests and rallies are likely in 1993, although any disturbances, riots or infringements of the peace may feel the full force of the law.

The year will also see some interesting developments taking place on the world stage. New politicians will come to the fore and several countries will see changes in their leadership. There is also a strong possibility of some regimes – particularly in the Middle East and the Third World – being subjected to coups. Some of these actions could be particularly bloody and even result in civil war.

Rooster years have also been marked by acts of violence against those in positions of authority. Attempts on the life of Pope John Paul and President Reagan were made in the Rooster year of 1981 and President Sadat was assassinated in that year. It is to be hoped that such acts of violence will not take place in 1993, but the threat cannot be ruled out.

New international trade agreements will be made over the year and significant political alliances will be formed, bringing many Western and Eastern nations yet closer together. It was in a Rooster year that the treaties establishing the Common Market came into force. In 1993 the Common Market is not only likely to expand further but also the countries in the community will move closer together in their alliance.

Another area which is likely to receive much attention

over the year is the well-being of the individual. Governments and health authorities will be laying even greater emphasis on the importance of regular exercise and healthy eating, and there will be many campaigns promoting improvements in life-style. Important new measures will be introduced improving safety standards, putting tighter controls on the preparation and sale of food, and furthering consumer rights.

In addition to this, many individuals will take positive action on a personal level to improve their physical fitness and appearance. New exercise courses will gain many followers and there will be renewed interest in jogging, aerobics, yoga and Tai Chi. The London Marathon was first held in a Rooster year and this interest in personal fitness and welfare will prove a lasting and beneficial aspect of the year. Outdoor pursuits in particular are likely to see a growth in popularity over the year and many will give more time to activities such as rambling, swimming, water sports and gardening.

The Rooster year is often an important and favourable year for royal families. Many royal families are likely to find themselves at the centre of some great pageants and memorable events. Both 1969, when millions watched the investiture of Prince Charles as Prince of Wales, and 1981, when he celebrated his marriage to Lady Diana Spencer were Rooster years. Queen Victoria also celebrated her Diamond Jubilee in a Rooster year and it was in yet another Rooster year that General Franco made the historic announcement that the Spanish royal family would be restored to the throne after his death. In 1993 there will certainly be some major events concerning royal families, and some of these events will generate world-wide interest.

This will also be quite an important year as far as sporting achievements are concerned. Several athletic records will be broken – both Sebastian Coe and Steve Ovett attracted much excitement in 1981 by setting new world records, once within 24 hours of each other – and several famous tournaments and sporting events are likely to yield major upsets. It will be a year when new and previously unknown sporting figures emerge and triumph over more established stars and when the lesser teams triumph over the more famous teams. For sporting enthusiasts, 1993 will be a very exciting year.

Generally, this will be a positive year and a year of practical achievements. It will be a year of potential and, by working hard, all signs can benefit from the Rooster's positive influence. Naturally some signs will fare better than others over the year, but I hope that in the chapters and appendix that follow I have indicated how each of the signs can get the best from this most interesting of years. I hope, too, that this will be a happy and a fulfilling year for you.

The Rat

31 January 1900 to	18 February 1901	*Metal Rat*
18 February 1912 to	5 February 1913	*Water Rat*
5 February 1924 to	24 January 1925	*Wood Rat*
24 January 1936 to	10 February 1937	*Fire Rat*
10 February 1948 to	28 January 1949	*Earth Rat*
28 January 1960 to	14 February 1961	*Metal Rat*
15 February 1972 to	2 February 1973	*Water Rat*
2 February 1984 to	19 February 1985	*Wood Rat*

The Personality of the Rat

Everything comes if a man will only wait.
– *Benjamin Disraeli: a Rat.*

The Rat is born under the sign of charm. He is intelligent, popular, and loves attending parties and large social gatherings. He is able to establish friendships with remarkable ease and people generally feel relaxed in his company. He is a very social creature and is genuinely interested in the welfare and activities of others. He has a good understanding of human nature and his advice and opinions are often sought.

The Rat is a hard and diligent worker. He is also very imaginative and is never short of ideas. However, he does sometimes lack the confidence to promote his ideas as much as he should and this can often prevent him from securing the recognition and credit he so often deserves.

The Rat is very observant and there are many who have made excellent writers and journalists. He also excels at personnel and PR work and any job which brings him into contact with people and the media. His skills are particularly appreciated in times of crisis, for the Rat has an incredibly strong sense of self-preservation. When it comes to finding a way out of an awkward situation, the Rat is certain to be the one who comes up with a solution.

The Rat loves to be where there is a lot of action, but should he ever find himself in a very bureaucratic or restrictive environment he can become a stickler for discipline and routine.

He is also something of an opportunist and is constantly on the look-out for ways in which he can improve his wealth and lifestyle. He rarely lets an opportunity go by and can become involved in so many plans and schemes that he sometimes squanders his energies and achieves very little as a result. He is also rather gullible and can be taken in by those less scrupulous than himself.

Another characteristic of the Rat is his attitude to money. He is very thrifty and to some he may appear a little mean. The reason for this is purely that he likes to keep his money within his family. He can be most generous to his partner, his children, and close friends and relatives. He can also be generous to himself, for he often finds it impossible to deprive himself of any luxury or object which he fancies. The Rat is also very acquisitive and can be a notorious hoarder. He hates waste and is rarely prepared to throw anything away. He can also be rather greedy and will rarely refuse an invitation for a free meal or a complimentary ticket to some lavish function.

The Rat is a good conversationalist, although he can occasionally be a little indiscreet. He can be highly critical of others – for an honest and unbiased opinion, the Rat is a superb critic – and sometimes will use confidential information to his own advantage. However, as the Rat has such a bright and irresistible nature, most are prepared to forgive him for his slight indiscretions.

Throughout his long and eventful life, the Rat will make many friends and will find that he is especially well-suited to those born under his own sign and those of the Ox, Dragon and Monkey. The Rat can also get on well with those born under the signs of the Tiger, Snake, Rooster, Dog and Pig, but the rather sensitive Rabbit and Goat will find the Rat a little too critical and blunt for their liking. The Horse and Rat will also find it difficult to get on – the Rat craves security and will find the Horse's changeable moods and rather independent nature a little unsettling.

The Rat is very family orientated and will do anything to please his nearest and dearest. He is exceptionally loyal to his parents and can himself be a very caring and loving parent. He will take an interest in all his children's activities and will see that they want for nothing. The Rat usually has a large family.

The female Rat has a kindly, outgoing nature and involves herself in a multitude of different activities. She is a superb hostess and will usually have a wide circle of very good friends. She is conscientious about the upkeep of her home and has superb taste in home furnishings. She is extremely supportive to the other members of her family and, due to her resourceful, friendly and persevering nature, can do well in practically any career she enters.

Although the Rat is essentially outgoing and something of an extrovert, he is also a very private individual. He tends to keep his feelings to himself and while he is not averse to learning what other people are doing, he resents anyone prying too closely into his own affairs. The Rat also does not like solitude and if he is alone for any length of time he can easily get depressed.

The Rat is undoubtedly very talented but more often than not he fails to capitalize on his many abilities. He has a tendency to become involved in too many schemes and chase after too many opportunities all at one time. If he were to slow down and concentrate on one thing at a time he could become very successful. If not, success and wealth may elude him. But the Rat, with his tremendous ability to charm, will rarely, if ever, be without friends.

The Five Different Types of Rat

In addition to the 12 signs of the Chinese zodiac, there are five elements and these have a strengthening or moderating influence on the sign. The effects of the five elements on the Rat are described below, together with the years in which the elements were exercising their influence. Therefore all Rats born in 1900 and 1960 are Metal Rats, those born in 1912 and 1972 are Water Rats, and so on.

Metal Rat: 1900, 1960
This Rat has excellent taste and certainly knows how to appreciate the finer things in life. His home is comfortable and nicely decorated and he is forever entertaining or mixing in fashionable circles. He has considerable financial acumen and invests his money well. On the surface the Metal Rat appears cheerful and confident, but deep down he can be troubled by worries that are quite often of his own making. He is exceptionally loyal to his family and friends.

Water Rat: 1912, 1972
The Water Rat is intelligent and very astute. He is a deep thinker and can express his thoughts clearly and persuasively. He is always eager to learn and is talented in many different areas. The Water Rat is usually very popular but his fear of loneliness can sometimes lead him into mixing with the wrong sort of company. He is a particularly skilful writer, but he can get side-tracked very easily and should try to concentrate on just one thing at a time.

Wood Rat: 1924, 1984
The Wood Rat has a friendly, outgoing personality and is

most popular with his colleagues and friends. He has a quick, agile brain and likes to turn his hand to anything he thinks may be useful. His one fear is insecurity, but given his intelligence and capabilities this fear is usually unfounded. He has a good sense of humour, enjoys travel and, due to his highly imaginative nature, can be a gifted writer or artist.

Fire Rat: 1936

The Fire Rat is rarely still and seems to have a never-ending supply of energy and enthusiasm. He loves being involved in the action – be it travel, following up new ideas, or campaigning for a cause in which he fervently believes. He is an original thinker and hates being bound by petty restrictions or the dictates of others. He can be forthright in his views, but can sometimes get carried away in the excitement of the moment and commit himself to various undertakings without checking what all the implications might be. He has a resilient nature and, with the right support, can often go far in life.

Earth Rat: 1948

This Rat is astute and very level-headed. He rarely takes unnecessary chances and, while he is constantly trying to improve his financial status, he is prepared to proceed slowly and leave nothing to chance. The Earth Rat is probably not as adventurous as the other types of Rat and prefers to remain in areas he knows rather than rush headlong into something he knows little about. He is talented, conscientious, and caring towards his loved ones, but at the same time can be self-conscious and worry a little too much about the image he is trying to project.

Prospects for the Rat in 1993

The Chinese New Year starts on 23 January 1993. Until then, the old year, the year of the Monkey, is still making its presence felt.

The year of the Monkey (4 February 1992 to 22 January 1993) is likely to have been a favourable year for the Rat and this is particularly so for the closing stages of the year. There will be opportunities to pursue and the Rat will be able to make considerable progress in many of his activities. However, in order to maximize these good trends, the Rat will need to maintain a persevering and determined manner. As the Chinese proverb goes, 'Perseverance makes all things easy.'

Socially, the latter part of the Monkey year will also be a happy time for the Rat. Many will have made some good friends over the year and for the single Rat, romance is particularly well aspected. There will be several most enjoyable functions for the Rat to attend near the end of the year and at one of these functions he could be given advice or receive some information which will prove most significant in the year ahead.

The one area of difficulty that could arise for the Rat is a conflict of opinion with someone, either in the home or at work. If such a situation occurs, the Rat should do all that he can to sort out the problem as quickly and as amicably as he can. To remain stubborn and obstinate – as some might be tempted to do – could cause problems for the future and also mar what will otherwise be a good year for the Rat. The final weeks of the year will also be a good time for him to complete any outstanding matters or correspondence that he might have.

The year of the Rooster starts on 23 January 1993 and is going to be a good year for the Rat, but it will also be a year of change. This could apply to his work or accommodation, and while it could be disruptive and cause the Rat some anxiety at the time, he can be assured that in the long run any changes that do occur will work out well for him. In many respects 1993 will be a most significant year, and the events that happen and progress the Rat makes will have an important bearing on the future.

In his work the Rat would do well to remain alert for new

opportunities to pursue. Many will be promoted or be given new responsibilities, and some Rats will be successful in broadening their experience by taking up a different type of work altogether. Rats seeking employment should pursue any opportunities that they see but would also do well to consider lines of work that they might not have contemplated before. By being persistent and to some degree adaptable, their efforts will be rewarded.

The Rat's family and social life will be generally happy and content over the year. Romance is again well aspected and the Rooster year is considered a favourable year for Rats to get married. There will be plenty of opportunities for the Rat to make new friends over the year and his social life, particularly in the spring and summer, is likely to be both busy and most enjoyable.

Domestically, 1993 will be eventful. Some Rats will change their accommodation altogether while others will make alterations to their property or garden. In either case, the Rat will find that this could cause considerable disruption, but he will be generally pleased with how things work out. However, should he feel under pressure or strain at any time of the year, he should not hesitate to ask his family and friends for assistance. He will find others most supportive and co-operative. Despite the generally busy nature of the year, however, 1993 will hold some most pleasurable moments. Many Rats can look forward to a personal celebration over the year or some extremely good news concerning a member of the family.

Although the year of the Rooster is generally a protected year for the Rat, he cannot afford to be complacent or take unnecessary chances. In financial matters in particular, the Rat will need to be careful and cautious. He should be wary of getting involved in any risky undertakings and would do well to keep a careful watch over his level of expenditure. Provided he is both prudent and cautious, he will not go far wrong.

Another area where the Rat needs to exercise care is with

his own well-being. Although he will generally enjoy good health in 1993, he cannot afford to take liberties or unnecessary risks. This is particularly true if the Rat undertakes any hazardous activity. Without due care and attention he could all too easily hurt himself and throughout 1993 he should remember the maxim 'It is better to be safe than sorry.'

There will be several opportunities for the Rat to travel over the year and the travelling that he does undertake will prove pleasurable. He will particularly enjoy visiting places he has not seen before and he should also take advantage of any opportunity to visit friends or relations he has not seen for some time.

Generally, 1993 will be a busy year for the Rat. There will be changes in store and many demands on his time. However, provided the Rat sets about his activities in a determined and organized manner, he will be pleased with what he is able to accomplish over the year and the considerable progress he will make.

As far as the different types of Rat are concerned, 1993 will prove a busy but memorable year for the **Metal Rat**. Over the year there will be numerous demands on his time and many matters which will require his attention. This applies to his family, his work and his various interests. In view of this, the Metal Rat should try to ensure that he sets about his various activities in a methodical manner and uses his time efficiently and effectively. He should guard against starting new commitments or projects which he does not have time to deal with properly and he would also be helped by establishing some idea of his priorities for the year. By being methodical and organized the Metal Rat will be truly delighted by what he is able to achieve, and his accomplishments over the year will be both considerable and significant. The Metal Rat can look forward to having some very pleasant times with his family and many Metal Rats will have cause for a personal celebration over the year. In his work he will make good progress and for those seeking employment or wanting to widen their experience, there will be several opportunities to pursue, particularly in the first half of the year. The Metal Rat will also be reasonably fortunate in financial matters although he would do well to keep a watch on his level of expenditure – sometimes he can be a little too extravagant and indulgent for his own good and he might be grateful for any money that he can set aside for better use in the future.

This will be a significant and memorable year for the **Water Rat**. Many Water Rats will get engaged or married or see an addition to their family and, on a domestic and social level, 1993 will be one of the best and happiest years the Water Rat has enjoyed for a long time. The year will, however, prove quite busy for the Water Rat and he may find that some of his longer term plans and aspirations will have to be rearranged. Nevertheless, he will be very pleased with his accomplishments over the year. In his work there will be some excellent opportunities to pursue and for those seeking employment, persistence and enterprise is likely to be rewarded. The Water Rat should also take advantage of any opportunities to widen his skills and experience – he will find that the knowledge he acquires over the year will do much to enhance his progress and prospects in the future. The Water Rat does need to be careful in financial matters in 1993 and should try to avoid getting involved in any risky or highly speculative ventures. He should also be wary of committing himself to too many activities at any one time, as putting himself under a lot of pressure could leave him tired and irritable, and sour what will otherwise be a most favourable and promising year for him.

This will be a generally enjoyable year for the **Wood Rat**. He can look forward to having some most pleasant times with his family and friends, and will also attend some enjoyable social functions over the year. There will be opportunities for him to travel and he will also be able to give much time and attention to his hobbies and interests. Any Wood Rat who may have been lonely in recent years or who would like additional interests would do well to go out more, join local societies or enrol on appropriate courses. If he does so, he will be very pleased he has made the effort and the new friends he makes or the new interests he takes up will be a great source of pleasure and happiness over the year. The Wood Rat does, however, need to deal with paperwork and official correspondence with care and he should also be wary about committing himself to any new financial undertaking unless he has checked the details carefully. Any Wood Rat who changes his accommodation in 1993 will find the move will work out well.

This will be an interesting and varied year for the **Fire Rat** and while not all the events of the year will work out as he had hoped, he will still be pleased with his achievements. The Fire Rat is likely to do well in his work and will continue to impress those around him with his energy and quick-thinking. Indeed, all Fire Rats would do well to pursue and promote any ideas that they have – they will find that these will be favourably received and that their reputation will be considerably enhanced. The Fire Rat should, however, be wary of adopting too much of an independent attitude over the year. If he does, he could find himself lacking support that could be useful to him later. This is more a year for joint rather than independent action. Should the Fire Rat experience any set-backs over the year, he should regard them as obstacles to overcome rather than defeats and, with a positive and determined outlook, he could even turn them to his advantage. This is also a good year for him to give some thought to his long-term future and it would be helpful for him to discuss his ideas with others. The ideas that he comes up with now could prove very useful to him in the next few years and indeed provide him with new goals to aim for. Domestic matters and travel are both well aspected and the Fire Rat will be much in demand with his family and friends. He will also derive much pleasure and satisfaction from his hobbies over the year.

This will be a significant and successful year for the **Earth Rat**. He can look forward to having some happy and memorable times with his family and friends, and he is likely to delight in a great success enjoyed by someone close to him. Domestically and socially this will be a good year for him, although the year will not be without its pressures and strains. Some Earth Rats will move or have alterations carried out to their property and this could prove disruptive and also quite costly. However, the Earth Rat will be well pleased with the final results. Many Earth Rats will also see changes connected with their work. They could be given additional responsibilities or be successful in obtaining a new and more challenging position. Some Earth Rats will also change the type of work they have been doing and while the change will at first appear daunting, they will be pleased with how things work out. Throughout 1993 the Earth Rat should act determinedly and not be afraid to act on his own initiative. The aspects are generally very favourable for him and his level of progress and success is in many ways dependent on his own degree of determination and positive outlook.

Famous Rats

Alan Alda, Dave Allen, Ursula Andress, Louis Armstrong, Charles Aznavour, Irving Berlin, Marlon Brando, Charlotte Brontë, George Bush, Lord Callaghan, Jimmy Carter, Pablo Casals, Dick Cavett, Raymond Chandler, Maurice Chevalier, Steve Cram, Barbara Dickson, Benjamin Disraeli, Elizabeth Dole, Noel Edmonds, T.S. Eliot, Ben Elton, Albert Finney, Sir Clement Freud, Clark Gable, Thomas Hardy, Vaclav Havel, Haydn, Charlton Heston, Benny Hill, Roy Hudd, Jeremy Irons, Glenda Jackson, Gene Kelly, F.W. de Klerk, Nastassja Kinski, Lawrence of Arabia, Ivan Lendl, Gary Lineker, Andrew Lloyd Webber, Lulu, Earl Mountbatten, Olivia Newton-John, Richard Nixon, Robert Palmer, Sean

Penn, Captain Mark Phillips, Enoch Powell, Prince, the
Queen Mother, Vanessa Redgrave, Burt Reynolds, Jonathan
Ross, Emma Samms, Ayrton Senna, William Shakespeare,
Wayne Sleep, Yves St Laurent, Tommy Steele, Shakin'
Stevens, James Taylor, Leo Tolstoy, the Prince of Wales,
Dennis Waterman, Roger Whittaker, Kim Wilde, the Duke
of York.

The Ox

19 February 1901 to	7 February 1902	*Metal Ox*
6 February 1913 to	25 January 1914	*Water Ox*
25 January 1925 to	12 February 1926	*Wood Ox*
11 February 1937 to	30 January 1938	*Fire Ox*
29 January 1949 to	16 February 1950	*Earth Ox*
15 February 1961 to	4 February 1962	*Metal Ox*
3 February 1973 to	22 January 1974	*Water Ox*
20 February 1985 to	8 February 1986	*Wood Ox*

The Personality of the Ox

Ideals are like stars; you will not succeed in touching
them with your hands. But like the seafaring man on
the desert of waters, you choose them as your guides,
and following them you will reach your destiny.
– Carl Schurz: an Ox.

The Ox is born under the signs of equilibrium and tenacity.
He is a hard and conscientious worker and sets about
everything he does in a resolute, methodical and determined manner. He has considerable leadership qualities
and is often admired for his tough and uncompromising
nature. He knows what he wants to achieve in life and, as
far as possible, will not be deflected from his ultimate
objective.

The Ox takes his responsibilities and duties very
seriously. He is decisive and quick to take advantage of any

opportunity that comes his way. He is also sincere and places a great deal of trust in his friends and colleagues. He is, nevertheless, something of a loner. He is a quiet and private individual and often keeps his thoughts to himself. He also cherishes his independence and prefers to set about things in his own way rather than be bound by the dictates of others or be influenced by outside pressures.

The Ox tends to have a calm and tranquil nature, but if something angers him or he feels that someone has let him down, he can have a fearsome temper. He can also be stubborn and obstinate and this can lead the Ox into conflict with others. Usually the Ox will succeed in getting his own way, but should things go against him, he is a poor loser and will take any defeat or set-back extremely badly.

The Ox is often a deep thinker and rather studious. He is not particularly renowned for his sense of humour and does not take kindly to new gimmicks or anything too innovative. The Ox is too solid and traditional for that and he prefers to stick to the more conventional norm.

His home is very important to him and in some respects he treats it as a private sanctuary. His family tends to be closely knit and the Ox will make sure that each member does their fair share around the house. The Ox tends to be a hoarder, but he is always well-organized and neat. He also places great importance on punctuality and there is nothing that infuriates him more than to be kept waiting – particularly if it is due to someone's inefficiency. The Ox can be a hard task master!

Once settled in a job or house the Ox will quite happily remain there for many years. He does not like change and he is also not particularly keen on travel. He does, however, enjoy gardening and other outdoor pursuits and he will often spend much of his spare time out of doors. The Ox is usually an excellent gardener and whenever possible he will always make sure he has a large area of ground to maintain. The Ox usually prefers to live in the country rather than the town.

Due to his dedicated and dependable nature, he will usually do well in his chosen career – providing he is given enough freedom to act on his own initiative. He invariably does well in politics, agriculture, and in careers which need specialized training. The Ox is also very gifted in the arts and there are many who have enjoyed considerable success as musicians or composers.

The Ox is not as outgoing as some and it often takes him a long time to establish friendships and feel relaxed in another person's company. His courtships are likely to be long, but once he is settled he will remain devoted and loyal to his partner. The Ox is particularly well-suited to those born under the signs of the Rat, Rabbit, Snake and Rooster. He can also establish a good relationship with the Monkey, Dog, Pig and another Ox, but he will find that he has little in common with the whimsical and sensitive Goat. He will also find it difficult to get on with the Horse, Dragon and Tiger – the Ox prefers a quiet and peaceful existence and those born under these three signs tend to be a little too lively and impulsive for his liking.

The lady Ox has a kind and caring nature and her home and her family are very much her pride and joy. She always tries to do her best for her partner and can be a most conscientious and loving parent. The lady Ox is an excellent organiser and she is also a very determined person who will often succeed in getting what she wants in life. She usually has a deep interest in the arts and is often a talented artist or musician.

The Ox is a very down-to-earth character. He is sincere, loyal and unpretentious. He can, however, be rather reserved and to some he may appear distant and aloof. He has a quiet nature, but underneath he is very strong-willed and ambitious. He has the courage of his convictions and is often prepared to stand up for what he believes is right, regardless of the consequences. He inspires confidence and trust and throughout his life he will rarely be short of people who are ready to support him or who admire his strong and resolute manner.

The Five Different Types of Ox

In addition to the 12 signs of the Chinese zodiac, there are five elements and these have a strengthening or moderating influence on the sign. The effects of the five elements on the Ox are described below, together with the years in which the elements were exercising their influence. Therefore all Oxen born in 1901 and 1961 are Metal Oxen, those born in 1913 and 1973 are Water Oxen, and so on.

Metal Ox: 1901, 1961
This Ox is confident and very strong-willed. He can be blunt and forthright in his views and is not afraid of speaking his mind. He sets about his objectives with a dogged determination, but he can become so wrapped up in his various activities that he can be oblivious to the thoughts and feelings of those around him, and this can sometimes be to his detriment. He is honest and dependable and will never promise more than he can deliver. He has a good appreciation of the arts and usually has a small circle of very good and loyal friends.

Water Ox: 1913, 1973
This Ox has a sharp and penetrating mind. He is a good organizer and sets about his work in a methodical manner. He is not as narrow-minded as some of the other types of Oxen and is more willing to involve others in his plans and aspirations. He usually has very high moral standards and is often attracted to careers in public service. He is a good judge of character and has such a friendly and persuasive manner that he usually experiences little difficulty in securing his objectives. He is popular and has an excellent way with children.

Wood Ox: 1925, 1985

The Wood Ox conducts himself with an air of dignity and authority and will often take a leading role in any enterprise with which he gets involved. He is very self-confident and is direct in his dealings with others. He does, however, have a quick temper and has no hesitation in speaking his mind. He has tremendous drive and will-power and has an extremely good memory. The Wood Ox is particularly loyal and devoted to the members of his family and has a most caring nature.

Fire Ox: 1937

The Fire Ox has a powerful and assertive personality and is a hard and conscientious worker. He holds strong views and has very little patience when things do not go his own way. He can also get carried away in the excitement of the moment and does not always take into account the views of those around him. He nevertheless has many leadership qualities and will often reach positions of power, eminence and wealth. He usually has a small group of loyal and close friends and is very devoted to his family.

Earth Ox: 1949

This Ox sets about everything he does in a sensible and level-headed manner. He is ambitious, but he is also realistic in his aims and is often prepared to work long hours in order to secure his objectives. He is shrewd in financial and business matters and is a very good judge of character. He has a quiet nature and is greatly admired for his sincerity and integrity. He is also very loyal to his family and friends and his views and opinions are often sought by others.

Prospects for the Ox in 1993

The Chinese New Year starts on 23 January 1993. Until then, the old year, the year of the Monkey, is still making its presence felt.

Over the course of the year of the Monkey (4 February 1992 to 22 January 1993) the Ox is likely to have seen several changes take place, as a Monkey year is often a year of change for the Ox. These changes could involve his work, his home or his general life-style, and while the Ox is never one who particularly relishes change, these will generally work out in his favour. Any Ox who still has misgivings about the events that have taken place can take comfort, as the year of the Monkey is in many respects a turning point, and some of the uncertainties and misgivings he may have had will almost certainly be displaced in the months ahead.

The Ox is also likely to have made new friends and acquaintances over the year of the Monkey and some of the contacts he has built up will prove extremely useful to him in the future.

Although the Ox will be kept fairly busy during the latter part of the Monkey year, he would do well to give some thought to his plans and hopes for 1993. He should use any opportunity that he has to complete outstanding matters or to finish any jobs which he might not have had time to complete over the year. He will be surprised at just how much he can accomplish at this time and he will then be able to turn his attention to the challenges and opportunities that the new year will bring.

The year of the Rooster starts on 23 January 1993 and is going to be a pleasing year for the Ox. After some of the events and changes that have taken place in recent times, the year of the Rooster will bring method and order back to his life and this is something the Ox will greatly appreciate and benefit from.

The year of the Rooster is an ideal time for the Ox to build on recent successes, put into practice any ideas that he has and to promote himself and his abilities. His progress over the year can be quite considerable and he will be heartened by the support and co-operation he is given by his family, friends and colleagues. This is a year when the Ox can act with resolute determination and reap the rewards for his efforts. Many Oxen will make progress in their work, be given new responsibilities or gain employment in a new and different type of job. In addition, anything that the Ox can do to widen his experience or to promote himself will be to his advantage. This is very much a year when the Ox will find much truth in the saying 'Seek and you will find.'

Naturally no year is without its problems and the Ox will, over the course of the year, have a few problems to deal with. However, these will not be serious and the Ox would do well to look at any problems that do occur as challenges to overcome and triumph over. By dealing with any set-backs or problems in his usual stout-hearted way, he will emerge from the year a wiser and more knowledgeable person and this can only be to his future good.

In addition to making progress in his work, the Ox will also have some happy times with his family and friends. His domestic life will be generally content, and he would do well to involve those close to him in his various ideas and projects. He will be truly grateful for the support he is given. The single Ox will also lead a happy social life over the year and there will be plenty of opportunities to meet others and make new friends. Matters of the heart are particularly well aspected in 1993.

The Ox does, however, need to be careful when dealing with financial matters. He should be wary of entering speculative ventures or of putting his money at risk. He should also avoid lending his money to others as he could experience difficulties in getting the loan repaid. Provided he is cautious, all will be well, but this is just not a year when the Ox can take risks in financial matters. If he does, the indications are that he could suffer financial loss and set-backs.

For those Oxen who move or change their accommodation over the year – as many will – vigilance and care is essential. The Ox should also resist being hurried or pressurized into making any decision against his better judgement. He would do well to check the terms and clauses of any transaction he enters very carefully and, if he has any doubts, he should seek reliable professional advice. Provided he is careful, his move will work out well for him.

One other area that the Ox will need to watch over the year is his own well-being. Despite his considerable stamina, he should not take liberties with his health. He would do well to ensure that he regularly sets a time aside for rest and relaxation, and eats a healthy and balanced diet. To drive himself relentlessly without taking proper care could leave him prone to colds and other minor ailments which, with good common sense, could be avoided.

There will be several opportunities for the Ox to travel over the year, in some cases over considerable distances. It is also a highly favourable year for visiting friends and relatives living some distance away and the Ox will certainly enjoy the travelling and holidays that he undertakes in 1993.

Generally, the year of the Rooster will be a pleasing year for the Ox. He will make considerable progress in many of his activities and at the same time lead a pleasant and enjoyable family and social life. Provided he is careful in financial matters and sets about his various activities in his usual sensible and level-headed manner, this will be a year he will be able to look back on with considerable satisfaction.

As far as the different types of Ox are concerned, 1993 will be a busy and challenging year for the **Metal Ox**. He will find events will move very much in his favour over the year and that he will be able to accomplish a great deal in most of his activities. He can look forward to making progress in his work and the year will present the Metal Ox with some excellent opportunities and interesting new challenges to pursue. For those seeking work, or wanting to widen their experience, 1993 is a year to go after new positions with resolution and determination. Should he meet with any set-backs or problems, the Metal Ox should show himself flexible and adaptable and yet, true to his own nature, remain as determined as ever. By being bold and determined he will secure his goals and make great progress. In addition to doing well in work matters, his domestic and social life will also be content and settled. He is likely to build up some new friendships over the year and his circle of contacts and acquaintances will widen appreciably. The Metal Ox does, however, need to be careful in money matters and should be wary of committing himself to any new and large financial undertaking unless he is sure that he can meet the costs involved. To stretch his resources too far could cause problems. In view of the many demands and pressures that the Metal Ox will experience over the year, he would also do well to make sure that he regularly sets some time aside for recreational pursuits, preferably something unrelated to his usual daytime activities. He should also ensure that he gets away for a proper break or holiday over the year.

This will be a successful and memorable year for the **Water Ox**. However, to maximize the auspicious trends, he should draw up some plan or have some idea of his objectives for the year. Without this there is a danger that he could drift through parts of the year, miss ideal opportunities and not realize his true potential. There will certainly be some interesting and challenging opportunities in his work and all Water Oxen will benefit by broadening their experience over the year and, if possible, increasing their skills. Socially and romantically, 1993 will be a splendid year and many Water Oxen will get engaged or married or see an addition to their family over the year. The Water Ox does, however, need to deal with matters concerning property and accommodation extremely carefully and keep a close watch on his expenditure. Without proper attention, he could find his general outgoings far greater than he had realized and this could lead to problems. This is a year for prudence.

Generally the Water Ox will be well pleased with his progress in 1993, and during the course of the year he will impress and win the admiration of many. In addition to this, the experience he gains will prove of great value and significance in the years ahead.

This will be a most important year for the **Wood Ox** and over the year he will make several decisions which will have an important bearing on his future. These decisions could concern almost any aspect of his life, but in dealing with them the Wood Ox would do well to seek the opinions of others and avoid making any irrevocable decisions on the spur of the moment. This particularly applies to any change in accommodation. The Wood Ox should take his time and not do anything against his better judgement. In the long run, he will be pleased with how the decisions and any action he takes will work out. The year will also give the Wood Ox opportunities to take up a new interest or to devote time to his hobbies, which are likely to be a great source of pleasure for him. Travel is also favourably aspected and the Wood Ox is likely to enjoy the travelling and any breaks and holidays that he takes. The year will also hold several pleasant surprises – the Wood Ox could enjoy success in a competition he enters and also meet some friends or relations he has not seen for many years.

This can be a year of progress for the **Fire Ox**, although the amount of progress he makes is partly dependent on his attitude and his willingness to co-operate with others. In 1993 he cannot afford to act either independently or to ignore the views of others. The year calls for concerted action and co-operation with those around him and, if he bears this in mind, he will find life much easier as well as enjoying a far greater degree of success. This will, however, be quite a busy year for him and he should be wary of taking on more tasks or responsibilities than he can sensibly handle at any one time. If he plans his activities in an orderly and efficient manner, he will be well pleased with what he is able to accomplish. The Fire Ox will make substantial progress in his work and he will also be fortunate in financial matters. If he does have any spare funds, a savings policy taken out over the year could prove a useful asset in years to come. Travel is also well aspected. The Fire Ox can look forward to having some splendid and memorable times with his family and friends over the year, and any Fire Ox who may have been feeling lonely in recent years will find that his social life will improve greatly over the year, particularly in the summer months.

This will be a busy and important year for the **Earth Ox** and he will be able to make substantial progress in many of his activities. There will be new opportunities to pursue and while some of these will bring change and moments of uncertainty, they will prove of lasting benefit to the Earth Ox. This is a year for the Earth Ox to be bold and to pursue his ambitions with a solid determination. He will generally find his family, friends and colleagues most supportive, and he should not hesitate to discuss his plans and hopes with others and to seek their advice on any matters that may be concerning him. He will be grateful and reassured by the support he is given. The Earth Ox will be generally fortunate in business and financial matters over the year although he would be wise to keep a close watch on his level of expenditure. He should also avoid any highly speculative or risky ventures or committing his money to anything without checking the facts beforehand. With the many demands on him over the year, he should also make sure that he sets sufficient time aside to devote to his family and for recreational activities. Indeed, if the Earth Ox is able to take up a new hobby or interest over the year, he is likely to find that this will be a great source of pleasure and will provide him with many hours of enjoyment and relaxation.

Famous Oxen

Johann Sebastian Bach, Warren Beatty, Tony Benn, Chuck Berry, Willy Brandt, Jeff Bridges, Benjamin Britten, Frank Bruno, Richard Burton, Barbara Bush, Johnny Carson, Barbara Cartland, Judith Chalmers, Charlie Chaplin, George Cole, Peter Cook, Bill Cosby, Tony Curtis, Sammy Davis Jr, Jacques Delors, Walt Disney, Patrick Duffy, Harry Enfield, Jane Fonda, Michael Foot, Gerald Ford, Peter Gabriel, Handel, King Harald V of Norway, Robert Hardy, Charles Haughey, Nigel Havers, Adolf Hitler, Dustin Hoffman, Anthony Hopkins, Billy Joel, Don Johnson, Jack Jones, King Juan Carlos of Spain, Mark Knopfler, Burt Lancaster, Jessica Lange, Angela Lansbury, Jack Lemmon, Nicholas Lyndhurst, John MacGregor, Barry McGuigan, Warren Mitchell, Robert Mugabe, Napoleon, Pandit Nehru, Paul Newman, Jack Nicholson, Oscar Peterson, Colin Powell, Robert Redford, Rubens, Ian Rush, Willie Rushton, Arthur Scargill, Monica Seles, Peter Sellers, Jean Sibelius, Valerie Singleton, Jimmy Somerville, Sissy Spacek, Bruce Springsteen, Meryl Streep, Loretta Swit, Margaret Thatcher, Twiggy, Mary Tyler Moore, Dick Van Dyke, the Princess of Wales, the Duke of Wellington, Alan Whicker, Ernie Wise, W.B. Yeats.

The Tiger

8 February 1902 to	28 January 1903	*Water Tiger*
26 January 1914 to	13 February 1915	*Wood Tiger*
13 February 1926 to	1 February 1927	*Fire Tiger*
31 January 1938 to	18 February 1939	*Earth Tiger*
17 February 1950 to	5 February 1951	*Metal Tiger*
5 February 1962 to	24 January 1963	*Water Tiger*
23 January 1974 to	10 February 1975	*Wood Tiger*
9 February 1986 to	28 January 1987	*Fire Tiger*

The Personality of the Tiger

Nothing great will ever be achieved without great men, and men are great only if they are determined to be so.
– *Charles de Gaulle: a Tiger.*

The Tiger is born under the sign of courage. He is a charismatic figure and usually holds very firm views and beliefs.

He is strong-willed and determined and sets about most of the things he does with a tremendous energy and enthusiasm. He is very alert and quick-witted and his mind is forever active. He is a highly original thinker and is nearly always brimming with new ideas or is full of enthusiasm for some new project or scheme.

The Tiger adores challenges and he loves to get involved in anything which he thinks has an exciting future or which catches his imagination. He is prepared to take risks and does not like to be bound either by convention or the dictates of others. The Tiger likes to be free to act as he chooses and at least once during his life he will throw caution to the wind and go off and do the things he wants to do.

The Tiger does, however, have a somewhat restless nature. Even though he is often prepared to throw himself wholeheartedly into a project, his initial enthusiasm can soon wane if he sees something more appealing. He can also be rather impulsive and there will have been occasions in his life when he has acted in a manner which he has later regretted. If the Tiger were to think things out or to persevere in his various activities, he would almost certainly enjoy a greater degree of success than he would otherwise obtain.

Fortunately the Tiger is lucky in most of his enterprises, but should things not work out as he had hoped, he is liable to suffer from severe bouts of depression and it will often take him a long time to recover. The Tiger's life often consists of a series of ups and downs.

The Tiger is, however, very adaptable. He has an adventurous spirit and rarely stays in the same place for long. In the early stages of his life he is likely to try his hand at several different jobs and he will also change his residence fairly frequently.

The Tiger is very honest and open in his dealings with others. He hates any sort of hypocrisy or falsehood. He is also well known for being blunt and forthright and has no hesitation in speaking his mind. He can also be most rebellious at times – particularly against any form of petty authority – and while this can lead the Tiger into conflict with others, he is never one to shrink from an argument or not stand up for what he believes is right.

The Tiger is a natural leader and can invariably rise to the top of his chosen profession. He does not, however, care for anything too bureaucratic or detailed and he also does not like to obey orders. He can be stubborn and obstinate and throughout his life he likes to retain a certain amount of independence in his actions and be responsible to no one but himself. He likes to consider that all his achievements are due to his own efforts, and unless he cannot avoid it he will rarely ask for support from others.

Ironically, despite his self-confidence and leadership qualities, the Tiger can be indecisive and will often delay making a major decision until the very last moment. He can also be sensitive to criticism.

Although the Tiger is capable of earning large sums of money, he is rather a spendthrift and does not always put his money to its best use. He can also be most generous and will often shower lavish gifts on friends and relations.

The Tiger cares very much for his reputation and the image that he tries to project. He carries himself with an air of dignity and authority and enjoys being the centre of attention. He is very adept at attracting publicity, both for himself and for the causes which he supports.

The Tiger often marries young and he will find himself best suited to those born under the signs of the Pig, Dog, Horse and Goat. He can also get on well with the Rat, Rabbit and Rooster, but will find the Ox and Snake a bit too quiet and too serious for his liking, and he will also get highly irritated by the Monkey's rather mischievous and inquisitive ways. The Tiger will also find it difficult to get on with another Tiger or a Dragon – both partners will want to dominate the relationship and could find it difficult to compromise on even the smallest of matters.

The Tigress is lively, witty and a marvellous hostess at parties. She is usually most attractive and takes great care over her appearance. She can also be a very doting mother and while she believes in letting her children have their freedom, she makes an excellent teacher and will ensure that her children are brought up well and want for nothing. Like her male counterpart, she has numerous interests and likes to have sufficient independence and freedom to go off and do the things that she wants to do.

She also has a most caring and generous nature.

The Tiger has many commendable qualities. He is honest, courageous and often a source of inspiration for others. Providing he can curb the wilder excesses of his restless nature, he is almost certain to lead a most fulfilling and satisfying life.

The Five Different Types of Tiger

In addition to the 12 signs of the Chinese zodiac, there are five elements and these have a strengthening or moderating influence on the sign. The effects of the five elements on the Tiger are described below together with the years in which the elements were exercising their influence. Therefore all Tigers born in 1950 are Metal Tigers, those born in 1902 and 1962 are Water Tigers and so on.

Metal Tiger: 1950

The Metal Tiger has an assertive and outgoing personality. He is very ambitious and, while his aims may change from time to time, he will work relentlessly until he has obtained what he wants. He can, however, be impatient for results and also get highly strung if things do not work out as he would like. He is distinctive in his appearance and is admired and respected by many.

Water Tiger: 1902, 1962

This Tiger has a wide variety of interests and is always eager to experiment with new ideas or go off and explore distant lands. He is versatile, shrewd, and has a kindly nature. The Water Tiger tends to remain calm in a crisis, although he can be annoyingly indecisive at times. He communicates well with others and through his many capabilities and persuasive nature he usually achieves what he wants in life. He is also highly imaginative and is often a gifted orator or writer.

Wood Tiger: 1914, 1974
The Wood Tiger has a very friendly and pleasant personality. He is less independent than some of the other types of Tiger and is more prepared to work with others to secure a desired objective. However, he does have a tendency to jump from one thing to another and can get easily distracted. He is usually very popular, has a large circle of friends and invariably leads a busy and enjoyable social life. He also has a good sense of humour.

Fire Tiger: 1926, 1986
The Fire Tiger sets about everything he does with great verve and enthusiasm. He loves action and is always ready to throw himself wholeheartedly into anything which catches his imagination. He has many leadership qualities and is capable of communicating his ideas and enthusiasm to others. He is very much an optimist and can be most generous. He has a likeable nature and can be a witty and persuasive speaker.

Earth Tiger: 1938
This Tiger is responsible and level-headed. He studies everything objectively and tries to be scrupulously fair in all his dealings. Unlike other Tigers, he is prepared to specialize in certain areas rather than get distracted by other matters, but he can become so involved with what he is doing that he does not always take into account the views and opinions of those around him. He has good business sense and is usually very successful in later life. He has a large circle of friends and pays great attention to both his appearance and his reputation.

Prospects for the Tiger in 1993

The Chinese New Year starts on 23 January 1993. Until then, the old year, the year of the Monkey, is still making its presence felt.

The year of the Monkey (4 February 1992 to 22 January 1993) could have been a frustrating year for the Tiger. Despite all his noble intentions, he could have found it difficult to make as much progress as he would have liked over the year and he could also have had some annoying problems and obstacles to overcome. However, towards the end of the Monkey year the Tiger will see a gradual improvement in his situation and this improvement will continue in 1993.

For the remaining months of the Monkey year, the Tiger should continue to set about his activities to the best of his abilities. He should involve others in his plans and not hesitate to seek the advice and support of those around him. He will find his progress will be much greater if he acts with the assistance and co-operation of others than if he maintains an independent stance, as some Tigers are apt to do. If he sees any particularly tempting opportunity, especially in work matters, the Tiger should act promptly and determinedly. His progress at this time can be quite considerable.

The Tiger would also do well to deal with any outstanding matters in the closing stages of the year and particularly sort out any disagreements or differences of opinion that might have arisen. To let any tensions or difficulties continue will only cause problems in the future and there will be many opportunities in the weeks leading up to the Christmas and New Year holidays to sort these differences out in an amicable and satisfactory manner.

There will also be opportunities for the Tiger to travel in the closing stages of the year and he can expect to lead a busy and pleasant social life at this time. He should also take advantage of any opportunity that he gets to rest and unwind, as the pressures and events of the year will have taken a lot out of him. Refreshed and revitalized, he will then be able to look forward to the interesting times that lie ahead for him.

The year of the Rooster starts on 23 January 1993 and is

going to be a significant year for the Tiger. He can expect
to make considerable progress in many of his activities, to
build on past achievements and generally to impress those
around him. However, to maximize his progress over the
year, the Tiger would do well to draw up a set of objectives
for the year and to have some idea of the things that he
would like to accomplish. Without some sort of plan, the
Tiger could easily drift through the year and not make the
best use of his considerable capabilities.

In his work, the Tiger can make substantial progress.
There will be new opportunities to pursue and the
prospects for obtaining a new job or of being promoted are
extremely favourable. However, throughout the year the
Tiger needs to remain aware of the feelings and views of
his colleagues, and in case of disputes or differences he
should be willing to compromise and fall in with others.
Sometimes the Tiger can be guilty of being intransigent and
also rather rebellious, and these traits can easily work
against him in the year of the Rooster. Those Tigers seeking
employment or a new position should also remain alert for
opportunities to pursue, particularly in the spring and
summer months. Such Tigers would do well to take
advantage of any opportunity that they get to widen their
skills and also consider types of work which they might not
have contemplated before. In general, by broadening his
skills and experience, the Tiger will do much this year to
sow the seeds for his future progress and success.

The Tiger will be fortunate in financial matters in 1993
and any monetary problems he might have been experiencing will be considerably eased during the year.
However the Tiger does still need to keep a close watch
over his general level of expenditure – particularly as he
can sometimes be too indulgent or generous for his own
good!

There will again be opportunities for the Tiger to travel
over the year and the travelling that he does undertake will
go well and prove most enjoyable.

Domestically and socially, the Tiger can also look forward to having some most pleasant times in 1993. However, he does need to involve those around him in his activities and, to preserve domestic harmony, he should avoid becoming too preoccupied with his own interests at the expense of the interests of others. It is, however, in this sphere of personal relations that the Tiger will need to take extra care throughout the year. Although he is always one for speaking his mind – and is often admired for his frankness and honesty – the Tiger would do well to remain diplomatic and tactful in any awkward situation or discussion in which he finds himself. Without care, he could easily upset others and this is something he should avoid at all costs. The Tiger may also have a few problems to overcome during the year. These are more likely to be irritating than serious, but the Tiger should exercise restraint when dealing with and overcoming any problems that he does face. He ought to look for ways to get round the problem and to seek compromise rather than confrontation. He will also find others around him will be co-operative and helpful over the year and he should not hesitate to seek their advice on any matter that might be bothering him. He will find the support he is given will prove most useful, and throughout the year he should remember that there are many who are prepared to help and assist him if he will let them.

There will be plenty of opportunities for Tigers who are unattached to make new friends and all Tigers will lead a pleasant social life. The spring and summer months are likely to be particularly happy and memorable.

Generally, this will be a pleasing and constructive year for the Tiger. He will make progress and, while there will be problems he will need to overcome, his gains can be quite considerable. He should remember though, that in most of what he does he needs to act with the support of others rather than independently. He would also do well to keep a close watch on his sometimes outspoken and rebellious nature. If he can do this, this will be a year of positive progress and one in which he will sow the seeds for yet further accomplishments in 1994.

As far as the different types of Tiger are concerned, 1993 will be a busy but generally rewarding year for the **Metal Tiger**. He will do well in most of his activities and provided he concentrates on specific objectives rather than wastes his energies on trying to do too much, he will obtain some very pleasing and worthwhile results. There will be new opportunities in his work and the Metal Tiger would do well to advance any new ideas that he has or, if he is seeking employment or wanting to widen his experience, to try to obtain a position which utilizes his skills in a new and more challenging way. The opportunities will be there, and with determination and his redoubtable character, the Metal Tiger is not only capable of achieving his objectives in the year but at the same time will impress many with his talents. He will also do well in financial matters over the year. Many Metal Tigers will spend much time in carrying out alterations to their property or garden, or even in moving. The Metal Tiger's social and domestic life will be most pleasant and although there will be many demands on his time, he should ensure that he does involve himself in the interests and activities of those around him. To become too preoccupied with his own interests will result in tension and strain. The travelling that he undertakes over the year will also be most enjoyable, but the one area that the Metal Tiger should particularly watch in 1993 is in the handling of any awkward problems that arise. He should not be too hasty in voicing his feelings or take any irrevocable action on the spur of the moment. If he does, he could regret his actions and this could mar what will otherwise be a generally favourable year for him.

This will be an interesting and stimulating year for the **Water Tiger**. Many new opportunities will be presented to him – particularly in his work – and he will go a long way towards bettering his current position and securing his goals and ambitions. Throughout the year the Water Tiger should set about his activities in a positive and determined way and advance any ideas he has. He may, however, have to contend with a few problems over the year and while these will not be serious, they will nevertheless enable the Water Tiger to show the true strengths and qualities of his character. In dealing with any problems that do arise in an effective and positive manner, he will win the respect and admiration of many and this will do much to enhance his reputation and future prospects. He should look at any problems that do arise as opportunities to overcome and triumph over. The Water Tiger will be generally fortunate in financial matters over the year and any spare funds that he can put towards his future, particularly by means of a long-term savings plan, will prove an excellent asset in years to come. His family and friends will give him much pleasure over the year and while he may not have as much time as he would like to devote to his various hobbies and interests, he should ensure that he allows himself the opportunity to rest and unwind at regular intervals over the year. He will also find any short breaks and holidays that he takes during 1993 will prove most enjoyable and beneficial for him.

This will be a year of change for the **Wood Tiger** and while it will not be without its problems, it will still prove a happy and generally enjoyable year for him. He will lead a good and active social life, and romantic matters are most favourably aspected. Many Wood Tigers will meet their future partner in the year or get engaged or married. There will also be change as far as work is concerned. Many Wood Tigers will move to a different and more interesting position over the year, and those seeking employment should pursue any opportunities that they see and also make every effort to contact those who may be in a position to help them. With determination their efforts will be rewarded. Any Wood Tiger involved in education will also do well, although it could prove in his interest to concentrate on specific subjects rather than be over-ambitious and try to accomplish too much at any one time. The Wood Tiger will, however, need to be prudent in financial matters over the year and not commit himself to any major financial undertaking without being sure of what all the obligations might be. Generally, however, the Wood Tiger will enjoy the year and provided he sets about his activities in a sensible and methodical manner, he can look forward to making much progress as well as enjoying himself at the same time.

This will be a relatively quiet year for the **Fire Tiger** and he will be able to devote himself to his hobbies, interests and family. He will lead a most pleasant domestic and social life and will be delighted in the success and achievements of a younger relation or a close friend. There will also be several opportunities for the Fire Tiger to travel over the year and it could prove an ideal time to visit relations or friends that he has not seen for some time. His travels will prove most enjoyable and give him much pleasure. Outdoor activities are also well aspected and for those Fire Tigers who enjoy following sport or who like walking, gardening or some other out-of-door activity, the year will hold many happy moments. The Fire Tiger does, however, need to be careful if he undertakes any strenuous activity, particularly if he has to move heavy objects, as there is a danger that he could strain himself and cause himself unnecessary suffering. He will be generally fortunate in financial matters over the year, although the one area that he does need to watch closely is any important correspondence or forms he receives. He needs to deal with these with great care and check the terms and the small print carefully. If in doubt, it would be worth his while getting sound professional advice.

This year will see a significant upturn in fortune for the **Earth Tiger**. If in recent years he has not been able to make as much progress as he would have liked, this will change in the year of the Rooster. There will be several opportunities for him to pursue and he should not hesitate to promote himself and his ideas. He will find those around him generally supportive and co-operative and, provided he maintains a determined and optimistic stance, he will be pleased with the progress he is able to make. There will be new openings to pursue in his work and many Earth Tigers can look forward to promotion or to obtaining a new and more lucrative position. The Earth Tiger will also lead a pleasant domestic and social life over the year. He could, however, be faced with several expenses in 1993, particularly as far as his property is concerned, and throughout the year he would do well to exercise restraint in his spending. Like the Fire Tiger, the Earth Tiger will obtain much pleasure from outdoor activities over the year and he is also likely to find much relaxation and enjoyment in a new hobby or an interest that he takes up.

Famous Tigers

Sir David Attenborough, Queen Beatrix of the Netherlands, Beethoven, Jon Bon Jovi, Richard Branson, Mel Brooks, Isambard Kingdom Brunel, Simon Cadell, Tommy Cannon, Agatha Christie, James Clavell, David Coleman, Phil Collins, Jason Connery, Alan Coren, Tom Cruise, Paul Daniels, Emily Dickinson, David Dimbleby, Isadora Duncan, Charles de Gaulle, Crystal Gayle, Mel Gibson, Goya, Sir Alec Guinness, Dwight Eisenhower, Frederick Forsyth, Bryan Gould, Elliott Gould, Sir Geoffrey Howe, William Hurt, Derek Jacobi, David Jacobs, Caron Keating, Matthew Kelly, Sarah Kennedy, Stan Laurel, Ian McCaskill, Ramsay Macdonald, Karl Marx, Marilyn Monroe, Eric Morecambe, Rudolph Nureyev, David Owen, Paganini, Jonathan Porritt, Marco Polo, Suzi Quatro, the Queen, Lionel Ritchie, Diana Rigg, Kenny Rogers, the Princess Royal, Sir Jimmy Savile, Phillip Schofield, John Smith (MP), Sir David Steel, Pamela Stephenson, Dame Joan Sutherland, Dylan Thomas, Julie Walters, Terry Wogan, Stevie Wonder.

The Rabbit

29 January 1903	to	15 February 1904	*Water Rabbit*
14 February 1915	to	2 February 1916	*Wood Rabbit*
2 February 1927	to	22 January 1928	*Fire Rabbit*
19 February 1939	to	7 February 1940	*Earth Rabbit*
6 February 1951	to	26 January 1952	*Metal Rabbit*
25 January 1963	to	12 February 1964	*Water Rabbit*
11 February 1975	to	30 January 1976	*Wood Rabbit*
29 January 1987	to	16 February 1988	*Fire Rabbit*

The Personality of the Rabbit

Let every dawn of the morning be to you as the beginning of life. And let every setting of the sun be to you as its close. Then let every one of these short lives leave its sure record of some kindly thing done for others; some good strength or knowledge gained for yourself.
– *John Ruskin: a Rabbit.*

The Rabbit is born under the signs of virtue and prudence. He is intelligent, well-mannered, and prefers a quiet and peaceful existence. He dislikes any sort of unpleasantness and will try to steer clear of arguments and disputes. He is very much a pacifist and tends to have a calming influence on those around him.

He has wide interests and usually has a good appreciation of the arts and the finer things in life. He also knows how to enjoy himself and will often gravitate to the best restaurants and night spots in town.

The Rabbit is a witty and intelligent speaker and loves being involved in a good discussion. His views and advice are often sought by others and he can be relied upon to be discreet and diplomatic. He will rarely raise his voice in anger and will even turn a blind eye to matters which displease him just to preserve the peace. The Rabbit likes to remain on good terms with everyone, but he can be rather sensitive and takes any form of criticism very badly. He will also be the first to get out of the way if he sees any form of trouble brewing.

The Rabbit is a quiet and efficient worker and has an extremely good memory. He is also very astute in business and financial matters, but his degree of success often depends on the conditions that prevail. He hates being in a situation which is fraught with tension or where he has to make quick and sudden decisions. Wherever possible he will plan his various activities with the utmost care and a good deal of caution. He does not like to take risks and does not take kindly to changes. Basically he seeks a secure, calm and stable environment, and when conditions are right he is more than happy to leave things as they are.

The Rabbit is conscientious in most of the things that he does and, because of his methodical and ever-watchful nature, he can often do well in his chosen profession. He makes a good diplomat, lawyer, shopkeeper, administrator or priest and he excels in any job where he can use his superb skills as a communicator. He tends to be loyal to his employers and is respected for his integrity and honesty, but if the Rabbit ever finds himself in a position of great power he can become rather intransigent and authoritarian.

The Rabbit attaches great importance to his home and will often spend much time and money to maintain and furnish it and to fit it with all the latest comforts – the Rabbit is very much a creature of comfort! He is also something of a collector and there are many Rabbits who derive much pleasure from collecting antiques, stamps, coins, *objets d'art* or anything else which catches their eye or particularly interests them.

The female Rabbit has a friendly, caring and considerate nature, and will do all in her power to give her home a happy and loving atmosphere. She is also very sociable and enjoys holding parties and entertaining. She has a great ability to make the maximum use of her time and, although she involves herself in numerous activities, she always manages to find time to sit back and enjoy a good read or a chat. She has a great sense of humour, is very artistic and is often a talented gardener.

The Rabbit takes considerable care over his appearance and is usually smart and very well turned out. He also attaches great importance to his relations with others and matters of the heart are particularly important to him. He will rarely be short of admirers and will often have several serious romances before he settles down. The Rabbit is not the most faithful of signs, but he will find that he is especially well-suited to those born under the signs of the Goat, Snake, Pig and Ox. Due to his sociable and easy-going manner he can also get on well with the Tiger, Dragon, Horse, Monkey, Dog and another Rabbit, but the Rabbit will feel ill-at-ease with the Rat and Rooster as both these signs tend to speak their mind and be critical in their comments – and the Rabbit just loathes any form of criticism or unpleasantness.

The Rabbit is usually lucky in life and often has the happy knack of being in the right place at the right time. He is talented and quick-witted, but he does sometimes put pleasure before work, and wherever possible will tend to opt for the easy life. He can at times be a little reserved and suspicious of the motives of others, but generally the Rabbit will lead a long and contented life and one which – as far as possible – will be free of strife and discord.

The Five Different Types of Rabbit

In addition to the 12 signs of the Chinese zodiac, there are
five elements and these have a strengthening or moderating
influence on the sign. The effects of the five elements on
the Rabbit are described below, together with the years in
which the elements were exercising their influence.
Therefore all Rabbits born in 1951 are Metal Rabbits, those
born in 1903 and 1963 are Water Rabbits, and so on.

Metal Rabbit: 1951
This Rabbit is capable, ambitious and has very definite
views on what he wants to achieve in life. He can
occasionally appear reserved and aloof, but this is mainly
because he likes to keep his thoughts and ideas to himself.
He has a very quick and alert mind and is particularly
shrewd in business matters. He can also be very cunning in
his actions. The Metal Rabbit has a good appreciation of the
arts and likes to mix in the best circles. He usually has a
small but very loyal group of friends.

Water Rabbit: 1903, 1963
The Water Rabbit is popular, intuitive and keenly aware of
the feelings of those around him. He can, however, be
rather sensitive and tends to take things too much to heart.
He is very precise and thorough in everything he does and
has an exceedingly good memory. He tends to be quiet and
at times rather withdrawn, but he expresses his ideas well
and is highly regarded by his family, friends and colleagues.

Wood Rabbit: 1915, 1975
The Wood Rabbit is likeable, easy going and very adaptable.
He prefers to work in groups rather than on his own and
likes to have the support and encouragement of others. He
can, however, be rather reticent in expressing his views and
it would be in his own interests if he could become a little
more open and forthright and let others know how he feels

on certain matters. He usually has many friends and enjoys an active social life. He is noted for his generosity.

Fire Rabbit: 1927, 1987

The Fire Rabbit has a friendly, outgoing personality. He likes socializing and being on good terms with everyone. He is discreet and diplomatic and has a very good understanding of human nature. He is also strong-willed, and provided he has the necessary backing and support he can go far in life. He does not, however, suffer adversity well and can become moody and depressed when things are not working out as he would like. The Fire Rabbit is very intuitive and there are some who are even noted for their psychic ability. He has a particularly good manner with children.

Earth Rabbit: 1939

The Earth Rabbit is a quiet individual, but he is nevertheless very shrewd and astute. He is realistic in his aims and is prepared to work long and hard in order to achieve his objectives. He has good business sense and is invariably lucky in financial matters. He also has a most persuasive manner and usually experiences little difficulty in getting others to fall in with his plans. He is held in very high esteem by his friends and colleagues and his views and opinions are often sought and highly valued.

Prospects for the Rabbit in 1993

The Chinese New Year starts on 23 January 1993. Until then, the old year, the year of the Monkey, is still making its presence felt.

The year of the Monkey (4 February 1992 to 22 January 1993) could have been a rather tricky year for the Rabbit and he is unlikely to have made as much progress as he would have liked. He could have found his plans frustrated and may also have had to contend with some worries, problems and delays.

For what remains of the year of the Monkey, the Rabbit should continue to set about his activities in his own conscientious manner, but at the same time make every effort to resolve any differences that might have arisen or overcome any problems that he might still have. The latter part of the year can be a most positive and constructive time for the Rabbit and indeed many Rabbits will achieve more in the closing stages of the year than in the earlier months.

Most Rabbits will thoroughly enjoy the Christmas and New Year holidays and many will make new friends and widen their circle of acquaintances at this time. Romance is also very well aspected and the single Rabbit in particular is likely to have an enjoyable social life in the closing months of the year. The Rabbit should, however, be wary of taking any financial risks in the year of the Monkey and would do well to keep a close watch on his outgoings. To stretch his resources too far could cause problems later.

The year of the Rooster starts on 23 January 1993 and is going to be a challenging year for the Rabbit. He will be able to make a modest amount of progress in most of his activities, but this progress will not be possible without much effort on his part.

As with last year, many Rabbits will have to contend with a few problems, but these are certainly not insurmountable and the Rooster year can still prove a most constructive year for the Rabbit. In addition, the experience that he gains over the year will help to lay the grounds for the progress he will make in the future. This year will also hold some very enjoyable times for him and so, despite the variable trends that may exist, it can still prove a most fulfilling and satisfying time for him.

Throughout the year, the Rabbit will need to work hard and pursue his objectives in a methodical and determined manner. He should avoid taking unnecessary risks or automatically assuming that he has the support of others. Indeed, throughout 1993 the Rabbit should make sure that he remains aware of the views of his family, friends and colleagues, and of all the developments going on around him. To keep himself to himself and remain aloof – as some Rabbits do – could leave him isolated and not receiving the support which he needs or deserves.

In his work, the Rabbit will need to proceed carefully and cautiously and make sure that he has the support of others before embarking on any major new enterprise. He should regard 1993 as a year for joint rather than independent action. There will, however, be opportunities to improve his position over the year and all Rabbits would do well to pursue any opportunities they see. The Rabbit could enjoy some good news concerning his work in May and June.

Financial matters also need to be handled with great care in 1993 and the Rabbit should be wary of committing himself to any highly risky or speculative venture. He should also be careful if he enters any large financial transaction over the year and would do well to be aware of all the obligations that he might be placed under. Provided he is his usual prudent and cautious self when dealing with money matters all will be well, but no Rabbit can afford to be complacent when dealing either with business or finance this year.

The Rabbit may also have to face a few obstacles and problems in the year and these could concern almost any aspect of his life. These problems are unlikely to be serious, however, and most can be dealt with by applying patience and good common sense. Also, when facing any problem, the Rabbit should look for ways in getting round the problem and, given his imaginative nature, he could easily surprise himself and others with some of his solutions. The one thing he should not do is to let any problem weigh down too heavily on him. He has some good friends he can turn to for advice and when in doubt he would do well to seek the advice of others.

On a more positive note, the Rabbit can look forward to having some most happy times with his family and friends. Domestic matters are well aspected and many Rabbits will see an addition to their family or be able to celebrate a personal achievement or that of someone close to them. The Rabbit will also derive much pleasure from his hobbies or interests over the year – especially if they involve him in outdoor activities. Any Rabbit who finds that he has spare time at his disposal should seriously consider taking up another hobby or interest. Likewise, those seeking friends or a more active social life should aim to go out more and, if possible, join a local club or society. The Rabbit will find that anything positive he can do – whether it is taking up a new interest or widening his circle of friends – will prove most beneficial for him. But he must make the effort in the first place.

There will also be opportunities for travel over the year, particularly in the late summer and the latter part of the year. Although not everything may go as well or as smoothly as he would like, this year can still prove a positive time for the Rabbit. His social and domestic life will be generally happy and the work that he does and the experience he gains will place him in good stead for the future. However, throughout the year, the Rabbit would do well to act in unison with others rather than trying to do things independently and on his own. Much of what the Rabbit does and accomplishes in 1993 will pave the way for the greatly improved trends that exist for him in 1994, the year of the Dog.

As far as the different types of Rabbit are concerned, 1993 will be an important year for the **Metal Rabbit**. Over the course of the year he will take several decisions which will have an important bearing on his long-term future. These decisions could concern either his work or his accommodation and before arriving at any firm conclusion, he would do well to seek the advice and opinions of those around him. He should also not allow himself to be hurried into taking irrevocable action. By taking his time, the decisions and actions that he does take will work out well for him. In addition to giving thought to his future, the Metal Rabbit may have a few problems to contend with and, while not serious, he should again discuss any worries that he has with those around him. Sometimes the Metal Rabbit can let worries and problems weigh down heavily on him and in 1993 in particular, he will find much support and comfort in the advice and assistance he is given by others. The Metal Rabbit will find the second half of the year a generally more favourable time for him than the first. The year will also be quite busy and demanding for him and he should allow himself the opportunity to regularly rest and unwind and to devote time to his own interests and recreational pursuits. He will also find several short breaks taken at different times of the year will prove most beneficial for him.

This will be both a challenging and potentially rewarding year for the **Water Rabbit**. Like all Rabbits, he will find that he will have some minor problems to overcome in the year and that the results he desires may not be as forthcoming as he would like. However, the work that he does over the year and the experience he gains will prove exceptionally useful in the future and will, in many ways, act as a springboard to his future success and prosperity. Throughout the year, the Water Rabbit would do well to try and broaden his experience and if time allows, obtain an additional skill and qualification. He should regard 1993 as a year for preparation and renewal and the following years as years of action, progress and achievement. The Water Rabbit will also be helped during the year if he involves others more in his activities and ensures that he has the support of those around him if he intends to embark on any major new enterprise. The Water Rabbit will lead a generally happy domestic and social life over the year, and he will find his circle of friends and acquaintances will increase quite substantially. The Water Rabbit needs to be prudent in financial matters in 1993 although, if he has been experiencing monetary problems in recent times, he will find these will be generally eased over the course of the year.

This will be a valuable year for the **Wood Rabbit**, not so much for what he achieves but for what he learns. During the year the Wood Rabbit will make a reasonable amount of progress in many of his activities, but he will find that he does have some obstacles and problems to overcome. None of these obstacles and problems will be insurmountable or necessarily serious, but by dealing with and overcoming them he will learn a lot about himself and others, and he will also gain a lot in experience and confidence. Indeed, the events of the year will do much to strengthen his character and to lay the foundation for his future progress. During the course of the year he should be ready to involve others in his plans and be willing to discuss his hopes and aspirations with those around him – he will be considerably heartened by the assistance and support he is given. The Wood Rabbit should not hesitate to pursue any opportunities that he sees over the year, particularly concerning work and academic matters and, even if he meets with an occasional set-back, he will find a persevering and determined stance will eventually bring success. The Wood Rabbit will lead a very pleasant social life over the year and there will be splendid prospects for making new friends and for meeting others. The Wood Rabbit will, however, need to deal with financial matters particularly carefully over the year and, as far as possible, should avoid taking any risks.

This will be a relatively pleasant year for the **Fire Rabbit**. He will obtain much pleasure from his family and friends, and his domestic life is likely to be both settled and content. He will also derive much satisfaction from his hobbies and interests, especially if they involve him in outdoor activities and allow him to meet others. Any Fire Rabbit wanting to take up an additional interest is likely to find creative pursuits such as writing, photography or painting particularly absorbing and rewarding. The travelling that the Fire Rabbit undertakes in 1993 will also go well, especially if it allows him to visit places he has not seen before. On a more cautionary note however, the Fire Rabbit does need to handle important paperwork and official forms with care and if he finds himself involved in any bureaucratic or financial matter which he is unsure about, he would do well to seek professional advice. He should also avoid getting involved in any particularly risky or speculative venture, as he could easily end up the loser. Any Fire Rabbit who intends to move or change his accommodation over the year will find that his plans will go well but that the whole process could be more time-consuming and costly than he originally anticipated.

To achieve the best results in 1993, the **Earth Rabbit** should give some thought to his objectives and to what he would like to achieve in the near future. If possible, he should discuss his thoughts with those around him. Then, with some plan in mind, he should set about achieving his objectives and follow up any opportunities he sees. Anything that can help bring the Earth Rabbit closer to his objective – such as obtaining a new skill or approaching those who are in a position to help him – could prove of vital importance to his future success. If the Earth Rabbit has any problems or matters that are troubling him, he will be very much helped if he confides in those around him and seeks their advice and assistance. The year will prove quite demanding for the Earth Rabbit and he would also do well to ensure that he allows himself time to relax, to be with his family and friends, and also to devote himself to recreational pursuits. To drive himself too hard, or put himself under too much pressure, could leave him weary and not achieving the results he desires. The Earth Rabbit will obtain much pleasure from travel and outdoor pursuits over the year, and while he cannot afford to take unnecessary risks in monetary matters, he could still be fortunate in a financial transaction or a long-term savings policy that he takes out over the year.

Famous Rabbits

Prince Albert, Cecil Beaton, Harry Belafonte, Ingrid Bergman, Melvyn Bragg, Lewis Carroll, Fidel Castro, John Cleese, Confucius, Kenny Dalglish, Peter Davison, Ken Dodd, Paul Eddington, Albert Einstein, Peter Falk, W.C. Fields, Jodie Foster, James Fox, David Frost, James Galway, Hans-Dietrich Genscher, Cary Grant, John Gummer, Sir Richard Hadlee, Oliver Hardy, Bob Hope, Whitney Houston, John Hurt, Clive James, David Jason, Gary Kasparov, Penelope Keith, Cheryl Ladd, Julian Lennon, Patrick Lichfield, Ali MacGraw, George Michael, Roger Moore, Malcolm Muggeridge, Brian Mulroney, Nanette Newman, George Orwell, John Peel, Eva Peron, Edith Piaf, Denis Quilley, John Ruskin, Ken Russell, Mort Sahl, Elisabeth Schwarzkopf, George C. Scott, Selina Scott, Terry Scott, Sir Walter Scott, Neil Sedaka, Georges Simenon, Neil Simon, Frank Sinatra, Dusty Springfield, Sting, Jimmy Tarbuck, Sir Denis Thatcher, J.R.R. Tolkien, Arturo Toscanini, Liv Ullman, Luther Vandross, Queen Victoria, Terry Waite, Orson Welles.

The Dragon

16 February 1904	to 3 February 1905	*Wood Dragon*
3 February 1916	to 22 January 1917	*Fire Dragon*
23 January 1928	to 9 February 1929	*Earth Dragon*
8 February 1940	to 26 January 1941	*Metal Dragon*
27 January 1952	to 13 February 1953	*Water Dragon*
13 February 1964	to 1 February 1965	*Wood Dragon*
31 January 1976	to 17 February 1977	*Fire Dragon*
17 February 1988	to 5 February 1989	*Earth Dragon*

The Personality of the Dragon

In the mountains of truth, you never climb in vain.
Either you already reach a higher point today, or you
exercise your strength in order to be able to climb
higher tomorrow.
– Friedrich Nietzsche: a Dragon.

The Dragon is born under the sign of luck. He is a proud
and lively character and has a tremendous amount of self-
confidence. He is also highly intelligent and very quick to
take advantage of any opportunities that occur. He is
ambitious and determined and will do well in practically
anything which he attempts. He is also something of a
perfectionist and will always try and maintain the high
standards which he sets himself.

The Dragon does not suffer fools gladly and will be quick
to criticize anyone or anything that displeases him. He can

be blunt and forthright in his views and is certainly not renowned for being either tactful or diplomatic. He does, however, often take people at their word and can occasionally be rather gullible. If he ever feels that his trust has been abused or his dignity wounded he can sometimes become very bitter and it will take him a long time to forgive and forget.

The Dragon is usually very outgoing and is particularly adept at attracting attention and publicity. He enjoys being in the limelight and is often at his best when he is confronted by a difficult problem or tense situation. In some respects he is a showman and he rarely lacks an audience. His views and opinions are very highly valued and he invariably has something interesting – and sometimes controversial – to say.

He has considerable energy and is often prepared to work long and unsocial hours in order to achieve what he wants. He can, however, be rather impulsive and does not always consider the consequences of his actions. He also has a tendency to live for the moment and there is nothing that riles him more than to be kept waiting. The Dragon hates delay and can get extremely impatient and irritable over even the smallest of hold-ups.

The Dragon has an enormous faith in his abilities, but he does run the risk of becoming over-confident and unless he is careful he can sometimes make grave errors of judgement. While this may prove disastrous at the time, he does have the tenacity and ability to bounce back and pick up the pieces again.

The Dragon has such an assertive personality, so much will-power and such a desire to succeed that he will often reach the top of his chosen profession. He has considerable leadership qualities and will do well in positions where he can put his own ideas and policies into practice. He is usually successful in politics, show business, as the manager of his own department or business, and in any job which brings him into contact with the media.

The Dragon relies a tremendous amount on his own judgement and can be scornful of other people's advice. He likes to feel self-sufficient, and there are many Dragons who cherish their independence to such a degree that they prefer to remain single throughout their lives. However, the Dragon will often have numerous admirers and there are many who are attracted by his flamboyant personality and striking looks. If he does marry, he will usually marry young and will find himself particularly well-suited to those born under the signs of the Snake, Rat, Monkey and Rooster. He will also find the Rabbit, Pig, Horse and Goat make ideal companions and will readily join in with many of his escapades. Two Dragons will also get on well together as they understand each other, but the Dragon may not find things so easy with the Ox and Dog as both will be critical of his impulsive and somewhat extrovert manner. He will also find it difficult to form an alliance with the Tiger, for the Tiger, like the Dragon, tends to speak his mind, is very strong-willed and likes to take the lead.

The female Dragon knows what she wants in life and sets about everything she does in a very determined and positive manner. No job is too small for her and she is often prepared to work extremely hard until she has secured her objective. She is immensely practical and somewhat liberated. She hates being bound by routine and petty restrictions and likes to have sufficient freedom to be able to go off and do what she wants to do. She will keep her house tidy but is not one for spending hours on housework – there are far too many other things that she feels are more important and that she prefers to do. Like her male counterpart, she also has a tendency to speak her mind.

The Dragon usually has many interests and enjoys sport and other outdoor activities. He also likes to travel and often prefers to visit places that are off the beaten track rather than head for popular tourist attractions. He has a very adventurous streak in him and providing his financial

circumstances permit – and the Dragon is usually sensible
with his money – he will travel considerable distances
during his lifetime.

The Dragon is a very flamboyant character and while he
can be demanding of others and in his early years rather
precocious, he will have many friends and will nearly
always be the centre of attention. He has charisma and so
much confidence in himself that he can often become a
source of inspiration for others. In China he is the leader
of the carnival and he is also blessed with an inordinate
share of luck.

The Five Different Types of Dragon

In addition to the 12 signs of the Chinese zodiac, there are
five elements and these have a strengthening or moderating
influence on the sign. The effects of the five elements on
the Dragon are described below together with the years in
which the elements were exercising their influence.
Therefore all Dragons born in 1940 are Metal Dragons,
those born in 1952 are Water Dragons, and so on.

Metal Dragon: 1940
This Dragon is very strong-willed and has a particularly
forceful personality. He is energetic, ambitious and tries to
be scrupulous in his dealings with others. He can also be
blunt and to the point and usually has no hesitation in
speaking his mind. If people disagree with him, or are not
prepared to co-operate, he is more than happy to go his own
way. The Metal Dragon usually has very high moral values
and is held in great esteem by his friends and colleagues.

Water Dragon: 1952
This Dragon is friendly, easy-going and intelligent. He is
quick-witted and rarely lets an opportunity slip by.
However, he is not as impatient as some of the other types

of Dragon and is more prepared to wait for results rather than expect everything to happen that moment. He has an understanding nature and is prepared to share his ideas and co-operate with others. His main failing, though, is a tendency to jump from one thing to another rather than concentrate on the job in hand. He has a good sense of humour and is an effective speaker.

Wood Dragon: 1904, 1964
The Wood Dragon is practical, imaginative and inquisitive. He loves delving into all manner of subjects and can quite often come up with some highly original ideas. He is a thinker and a doer and has sufficient drive and commitment to put many of his ideas into practice. He is more diplomatic than some of the other types of Dragon and has a good sense of humour. He is very astute in business matters and can also be most generous.

Fire Dragon: 1916, 1976
This Dragon is ambitious, articulate and has a tremendous desire to succeed. He is a hard and conscientious worker and is often admired for his integrity and forthright nature. He is very strong-willed and has considerable leadership qualities. He can, however, rely a bit too much on his own judgement and not take into account the views and feelings of others. He can also be rather aloof and it would certainly be in his own interests to let others join in more with his various activities. The Fire Dragon usually gets much enjoyment from music, literature and the arts.

Earth Dragon: 1928, 1988
The Earth Dragon tends to be quieter and more reflective than some of the other types of Dragon. He has a wide variety of interests and is keenly aware of what is going on around him. He also has clear objectives and usually has no problems in obtaining support and backing for any of his ventures. He is very astute in financial matters and is often

able to accumulate considerable wealth. He is a good organizer although he can at times be rather bureaucratic and fussy. He mixes well with others and has a large circle of friends.

Prospects for the Dragon in 1993

The Chinese New Year starts on 23 January 1993. Until then, the old year, the year of the Monkey, is still making its presence felt.

The year of the Monkey (4 February 1992 to 22 January 1993) is likely to have been a reasonably good year for the Dragon, and this is particularly true for the latter part of the year.

Over the course of the year the Dragon will have made progress in many of his activities as well as impressing those around him. His ideas are likely to have been favourably received and he will have been able to accomplish things with relative ease. However, despite the generally favourable trends that exist for the Dragon in the Monkey year, he cannot afford to be lulled into a false sense of complacency. At all times the Dragon needs to pay close attention to what is going on around him and involve others in his various activities. If he takes risks or tries to do too much single-handedly, he could find himself in unexpected difficulties. The Dragon would, however, do well to go after any opportunities that he sees in the closing stages of the year – particularly as far as his work is concerned. He should also give some thought to his future and to the way he would like to see his career and life developing over the next year. Any thoughts and plans that he draws up could prove of more significance than he may realize at the time. On a more cautionary note, the Dragon does have to be careful in financial matters, particularly in the closing months of the year. He would be wise not to get involved in any highly speculative venture or to take risks with his money. He should also keep a close watch over his level of expenditure – he could find this much greater than he originally thought and, without care, this could lead to problems later.

The year of the Monkey will have been a demanding year for the Dragon and he should try to use any opportunity that he can get over the holiday period to rest and unwind and to prepare himself for the greatly improved trends that lie ahead.

The year of the Rooster starts on 23 January 1993 and is going to be a most auspicious year for the Dragon. He will do well in most of his activities and, true to his sign, he will be blessed with a certain amount of luck throughout the year.

The Dragon will make considerable progress in his career this year and many will move to a better and more lucrative position. Indeed, throughout 1993 the Dragon would do well to look out for opportunities to pursue and for ways in which he can advance his career. Whether he is seeking work, promotion or switching to a completely different type of job, the Dragon should move confidently and assertively. There will be several excellent opportunities for him – some occurring very early on in 1993 – which he can turn to his advantage.

In addition to doing well in his career, financial matters are also well aspected and any Dragon who may have been experiencing financial problems will find these eased over the year. Should the Dragon find himself with any spare money he would do well to consider taking out a savings policy or making an investment which would make provision for his long-term future. This could prove to be an excellent asset in years to come.

The Dragon is also likely to travel considerable distances in 1993, sometimes at short notice. The journeys that he does undertake will generally go well and he will also thoroughly enjoy any holiday or short breaks that he takes over the year.

The Dragon's domestic life will be generally content and he can look forward to having some good times with his family and friends. There is, however, an indication that many Dragons will move or consider moving over the year and, while in the long-term any change in accommodation will work out well for him, the actual process of moving could prove more time-consuming and costly than he originally envisaged.

There will be plenty of opportunities for the single Dragon to meet others over the year and while romance is generally well aspected, to avoid possible disappointment the Dragon should try not to build up high expectations from just a short friendship. He would do better to let the relationship develop naturally and in its own time.

The Dragon's social life will be most pleasant and many Dragons will make some new and very good friends during the year.

The Dragon will also derive considerable pleasure from his hobbies and interests in 1993, and the year is also favourable for taking up a new interest or for learning an additional skill. Anything that the Dragon can do to broaden his interests or experience could prove particularly beneficial for him in the future.

Naturally no year is without its problems, but the problems that the Dragon does experience in 1993 are unlikely to be serious and can be quickly dealt with. Should the Dragon have a clash of opinion with anyone, he would do well to resolve the matter as quickly and as amicably as he can. To let any disagreement linger in the background could mar what will otherwise be a splendid year for him and divert his energies from more profitable activities. He should also be particularly careful over important correspondence and official forms that he has to complete. A mistake or oversight could prove detrimental to him and take some time to sort out.

Generally, this will be a very pleasant year for the Dragon, and he should set about achieving his aims and ambitions with his usual solid determination. He would do well to promote his ideas and go after the opportunities that he will undoubtedly see. This will be a good and prosperous year for him and it rests with the Dragon to take advantage of the most favourable trends that exist for him.

As far as the different types of Dragon are concerned, 1993 will be a successful year for the **Metal Dragon**. If, in recent years, he has felt that his efforts have not received the recognition he feels they deserve, this will change in 1993. Those around him will be more amenable towards his ideas and projects and he will be able to make progress in most of his activities. In his work he should go after any opportunities that he sees and many Metal Dragons will be given greater responsibilities as the year progresses. Those Metal Dragons seeking work should particularly remain alert for ways in which they can use their skills, and with persistence their efforts will be rewarded. The trends for all Metal Dragons are most encouraging and he should act positively and determinedly throughout the year. The Metal Dragon will also enjoy good luck in financial matters as well as having the opportunity to travel. Socially too, this will be an active year and most Metal Dragons will find their circle of friends and acquaintances will widen as the year progresses. The Metal Dragon's home life will also be content and many will have good cause for a big family celebration over the year.

This will be a satisfying year for the **Water Dragon**. He is likely to make considerable progress in his work and many Water Dragons will transfer to a more responsible and lucrative position over the year. The Water Dragon will find that others will look favourably on his ideas and this is very much a time when he should pursue his objectives with a positive determination and bring his talents to the notice of others. The achievements of the Water Dragon can be quite considerable, but a lot does depend on his willingness to assert himself and to go after the opportunities that he sees. His family and friends will give him great pleasure over the year. If, however, he has any problems that are troubling him he should not hesitate to discuss them with others. Help and advice is all around him and he will be considerably heartened by the support and assistance he is given over the year. He will also be fortunate in financial matters in 1993 although many Water Dragons could incur some expense connected with their accommodation – either by carrying out improvements or moving. In either case, the Water Dragon would do well to keep a close watch on all the expenses involved and provided he is his usual careful and prudent self when dealing with money matters, he should end the year in a much improved financial position. There will be opportunities to travel over the year and for any Water Dragon who may have been lonely in recent years, the prospects for making new friends are favourably aspected. Indeed all Water Dragons will build up new friendships and contacts over the year and socially this will be a good year for him.

This will be a splendid and most enjoyable year for the **Wood Dragon**. He will be able to make considerable progress in many of his activities as well as leading a happy domestic life. The Wood Dragon will do very well in his work. He will continue to impress those around him and all Wood Dragons would do well to pursue any opportunities that they see and advance any ideas that they have. With determination and a positive outlook, the Wood Dragon can achieve a considerable amount over the year. Any Wood Dragon seeking work or wanting a change in his career would do well to follow up any openings that he sees and also to investigate types of work that he might not have fully considered before. By broadening his experience and skills, the Wood Dragon will do much to strengthen his career and lay the foundations for his future success. The Wood Dragon will also lead a pleasant social life over the year and he will meet and impress some who carry much influence and who can do much to help his future prospects. The Wood Dragon will obtain considerable pleasure from his family over the year, although he could be called upon to assist a relation or close friend who has an awkward problem. The time and attention he is able to give to this will be thoroughly appreciated. The Wood Dragon will be generally fortunate in financial matters but he should still be wary of stretching his resources too far or of getting involved in any particularly risky enterprise.

This will be an important and relatively successful year for the **Fire Dragon**. However to maximize the favourable trends that exist, he should have some idea of what he would like to achieve over the year and if possible draw up a set of priorities. He would also do well to discuss his ideas and plans with others and speak to those with experience. Then, with some idea in mind – whether it concerns his personal life, academic matters or his career – he should pursue his objective in his usual determined way. His progress, particularly as far as his career and academic achievements are concerned, can be quite considerable, but the Fire Dragon should first be sure in his mind what it is he wants to achieve. He should also not be too hasty or impatient for results. Time is on his side and the progress he makes in 1993 will give him a solid foundation on which to build in the future. The Fire Dragon will lead an active social life over the year and will make some new and very good friends. He does, however, need to watch his level of expenditure carefully over the year, although he could find his financial position considerably improved from the summer months onwards.

This will be a generally pleasant year for the **Earth Dragon**. He will have some particularly memorable times with his family and friends and is likely to be delighted at the achievements of someone very close to him. He will lead a pleasurable social life and attend some most interesting functions. There will also be opportunities to travel in 1993 and the holidays and short breaks that he does take will prove both enjoyable and beneficial for him. Many Earth Dragons will consider changing their accommodation over the year and this is likely to work out well for them. Business and financial matters are also well aspected, but the Earth Dragon should keep a close watch on his outgoings and avoid stretching his resources too far. It is also a good year for any Earth Dragon with creative skills, and he would do well to bring his talents to the attention of others. His work will be favourably received and, in some cases, could also prove quite remunerative. He will also enjoy outdoor pursuits, and those Earth Dragons who enjoy gardening or walking or who follow sport can look forward to having many satisfying moments over the year.

Famous Dragons

Jenny Agutter, Moira Anderson, Jeffrey Archer, Joan Baez, Peter Barkworth, Roseanne Barr, Count Basie, Simon Bates, Stanley Baxter, Saint Bernadette, Geoff Boycott, Tim Brooke-Taylor, Sir Alastair Burnet, Jennifer Capriati, Neneh Cherry, Kenneth Clarke, James Coburn, Bing Crosby, Roald Dahl, Salvador Dali, Robert De Niro, Susan Dey, Neil Diamond, Matt Dillon, Placido Domingo, Val Doonican, Faye Dunaway, Prince Edward, Bruce Forsyth, Michael Gambon, Sir John Gielgud, Graham Greene, Che Guevara, Edward Heath, James Herriot, Gloria Hunniford, Joan of Arc, Tom Jones, Martin Luther King, Bonnie Langford, John Lennon, Gina Lollobrigida, Queen Margrethe II of Denmark, Yehudi Menuhin, François Mitterrand, Bob Monkhouse, Desmond Morris, Johnny Morris, Hosni Mubarak, Florence Nightingale, Elaine Paige, Gregory Peck, Richard Pryor, Esther Rantzen, Christopher Reeve, Cliff Richard, George Bernard Shaw, Eduard Shevardnadze, Mel Smith, Ringo Starr, Princess Stephanie of Monaco, Karlheinz Stockhausen, Shirley Temple, Christopher Timothy, Lord Wilson of Rievaulx (Harold Wilson).

The Snake

4 February 1905 to	24 January 1906	*Wood Snake*
23 January 1917 to	10 February 1918	*Fire Snake*
10 February 1929 to	29 January 1930	*Earth Snake*
27 January 1941 to	14 February 1942	*Metal Snake*
14 February 1953 to	2 February 1954	*Water Snake*
2 February 1965 to	20 January 1966	*Wood Snake*
18 February 1977 to	6 February 1978	*Fire Snake*
6 February 1989 to	26 January 1990	*Earth Snake*

The Personality of the Snake

Just trust yourself, then you will know how to live.
– *Johann Wolfgang von Goethe: a Snake.*

The Snake is born under the sign of wisdom. He is highly intelligent and his mind is forever active. He is always planning and always looking for ways in which he can use his considerable skills. He is a deep thinker and likes to meditate and reflect.

Many times during his life he will shed one of his famous Snake skins and take up new interests or start a completely different job. The Snake enjoys a challenge, and he rarely makes mistakes. He is a skilful organizer, has considerable business acumen, and is usually lucky in money matters. Most Snakes are financially secure in their later years provided they do not gamble – the Snake has the distinction of being the worst gambler in the whole of the Chinese zodiac!

The Snake generally has a calm and placid nature and prefers the quieter things in life. He does not like to be in a frenzied atmosphere and hates being hurried into making a quick decision. He also does not like interference in his affairs and tends to rely on his own judgement rather than listen to advice.

The Snake can at times appear solitary. He is quiet, reserved, and sometimes has difficulty in communicating with others. He has little time for idle gossip and will certainly not suffer fools gladly. He does, however, have a good sense of humour, and this is particularly appreciated in times of crisis.

The Snake is certainly not afraid of hard work and is thorough in all that he does. He is very determined and can occasionally be ruthless in order to achieve his aims. His confidence, will-power and quick thinking usually ensure his success, but should he fail it will often take a long time for him to recover. He cannot bear failure and is a very bad loser.

The Snake can also be evasive and does not willingly let people into his confidence. This secrecy and distrust can sometimes work against him and it is a trait which all Snakes should try to overcome.

Another characteristic of the Snake is his tendency to rest after any sudden or prolonged bout of activity. He burns up so much nervous energy that without proper care he can - if he is not careful - be susceptible to high blood pressure and nervous disorders.

It has sometimes been said that the Snake is a late starter in life and this is mainly because it often takes him a while to find a job with which he is genuinely happy. However the Snake will usually do well in any position which involves research and writing and where he is given sufficient freedom to develop his own ideas and plans. He makes a good teacher, politician, personnel manager and social adviser.

The Snake chooses his friends carefully and, while he

keeps a tight control over his finances, he can be particularly generous to those he likes. He will think nothing of buying expensive gifts or treating his friends or loved ones to the best theatre seats in town. In return he demands loyalty. The Snake is very possessive and he can become extremely jealous and hurt if he finds his trust has been abused.

The Snake is also renowned for his good looks and is never short of admirers. The female Snake in particular is most alluring. She has style, grace and excellent (and usually expensive) taste in clothes. A keen socializer, she is likely to have a wide range of friends and has a happy knack of impressing those who matter. She has numerous interests and her advice and opinions are often highly valued. She is generally a calm-natured person and while she involves herself in many activities, she likes to retain a certain amount of privacy in the things that she does.

The affairs of the heart are very important to the Snake and he will often have many romances before he finally settles down. He will find that he is particularly well suited to those born under the signs of the Ox, Dragon, Rabbit and Rooster. Provided the Snake is allowed sufficient freedom to pursue his own interests he can also build up a very satisfactory relationship with the Rat, Horse, Goat, Monkey and Dog, but he should try to steer clear of another Snake as they could very easily become jealous of each other. The Snake will also have difficulty in getting on with the honest and down-to-earth Pig, and will find the Tiger far too much of a disruptive influence on his quiet and peace-loving ways.

The Snake certainly appreciates the finer things in life. He enjoys good food and often takes a keen interest in the arts. He also enjoys reading and is invariably drawn to subjects such as philosophy, political thought, religion or the occult. He is fascinated by the unknown and his enquiring mind is always looking for answers. Some of the world's most original thinkers have been Snakes, and –

although he may not readily admit it – the Snake is often psychic and relies a lot on intuition.

The Snake is certainly not the most energetic member of the Chinese zodiac. He prefers to proceed at his own pace and to do the things he wants. He is very much his own master and throughout his life he will try his hand at many things. The Snake is something of a dabbler, but at some time – and usually when he least expects it – his hard work and his efforts will be recognized and he will invariably meet with the success and the financial security which he so much desires.

The Five Different Types of Snake

In addition to the 12 signs of the Chinese zodiac, there are five elements and these have a strengthening or moderating influence on the sign. The effects of the five elements on the Snake are described below together with the years in which the elements were exercising their influence. Therefore all Snakes born in 1941 are Metal Snakes, those born in 1893 and 1953 are Water Snakes, and so on.

Metal Snake: 1941
This Snake is quiet, confident and fiercely independent. He often prefers to work on his own and will only let a privileged few into his confidence. He is quick to spot opportunities and will set about achieving his objectives with an awesome determination. He is astute in financial matters and will often invest his money well. He also has a liking for the finer things in life and has a good appreciation of the arts, literature, music and good food. He usually has a small group of extremely good friends and can be generous to his loved ones.

Water Snake: 1893, 1953
This Snake has a wide variety of interests. He enjoys

studying all manner of subjects and is capable of undertaking quite detailed research and becoming a specialist in his chosen area. He is highly intelligent, has a good memory, and is particularly astute when dealing with business and financial matters. He tends to be quietly spoken and a little reserved, but he does have sufficient strength of character to make his views known and attain his ambitions. He is very loyal to his family and friends.

Wood Snake: 1905, 1965
The Wood Snake has a friendly temperament and a good understanding of human nature. He is able to communicate well with others and often has many friends and admirers. He is witty, intelligent and ambitious. He has numerous interests and prefers to live in a quiet, stable environment where he can work without too much interference. He enjoys the arts and usually derives much pleasure from collecting paintings and antiques. His advice – particularly on social and domestic matters – is often very highly valued.

Fire Snake: 1917, 1977
The Fire Snake tends to be more forceful, outgoing and energetic than some of the other types of Snake. He is ambitious, confident and never slow in voicing his opinions – and he can be very abrasive to those he does not like. He does, however, have many leadership qualities and can win the respect and support of many with his firm and resolute manner. He usually has a good sense of humour, a wide circle of friends and a very active social life. The Fire Snake is also a keen traveller.

Earth Snake: 1929, 1989
The Earth Snake is charming, amusing, and has a very amiable manner. He is conscientious and reliable in his work and approaches everything he does in a level-headed and sensible way. He can, however, tend to err on the

cautious side and never likes to be hassled into making a decision. He is extremely adept in dealing with financial matters and is a shrewd investor. He has many friends and is very supportive towards the members of his family.

Prospects for the Snake in 1993

The Chinese New Year starts on 23 January 1993. Until then, the old year, the year of the Monkey, is still making its presence felt.

The year of the Monkey (4 February 1992 to 22 January 1993) is likely to have been a mixed year for the Snake. He could have found it difficult to make as much progress as he would have liked and may also have had some problems – particularly of a bureaucratic nature – to contend with.

However, although his progress may have been disappointing, the Snake can take heart. Generally, the latter part of the Monkey year will be a much more favourable time for him. He will find progress a little easier and those around him more accommodating about his views, plans and ideas. He could also have some encouraging news about his work and finances at this time.

A Monkey year is an ideal year for the Snake to widen his experience, obtain further qualifications or pursue cultural activities, and anything that the Snake can do in this direction is likely to be both rewarding and beneficial for him. In many respects, the work that the Snake does and the experience that he gains at this time will serve him extremely well in 1993, the year of the Rooster.

Domestically and socially, the year of the Monkey will have been a generally favourable year for the Snake and he can look forward to having some very pleasant times with his family and friends around the Christmas and New Year holidays. He should also take advantage of any opportunity that he has to rest and unwind and build up his energies for the forthcoming year. The Monkey year will have been a demanding and tiring time for him, but refreshed and revitalized, the Snake will be better placed to take advantage of the exciting prospects that now await him.

The year of the Rooster starts on 23 January 1993 and will be a most auspicious year for the Snake. He will be able to make unprecedented progress in many of his activities and be able to reap the rewards of his past efforts.

The Snake will do especially well in his work. If he is seeking a new job or promotion or is thinking of setting up his own business, he will be able to proceed with confidence. He will find others will look favourably on his ideas and he should promote his talents as much as he can. Sometimes the Snake loses out on opportunities because he is not assertive enough, and in 1993 all Snakes would do well to make a concerted effort to improve their position and status. The aspects are most favourable, and throughout the year the Snake should be bold, positive and determined.

Despite the likely good fortune in his career, the Snake cannot, however, be complacent in financial matters. Although many will find their financial position will improve over the year, Snakes cannot afford to lose their hard-earned gains by a careless investment or by squandering their money away needlessly. This is a year for financial care and restraint in the Snake's general level of spending.

The Snake's home life, however, is very well aspected. Those around him will be most supportive and encouraging and most Snakes will lead a content and happy home life. The Snake's family will be a great source of pride to him, although if at any time he feels concerned about a close relation or some domestic matter, he should let his concern be known rather than conceal his feelings. He may also need to give some assistance to someone close to him over the year and although it may prove a difficult matter, the advice he gives will be of great value.

The Snake will lead a pleasant social life in 1993. He will

attend some interesting and enjoyable social occasions and all Snakes will find that their circle of friends and acquaintances increases over the year. Those Snakes who have a tendency to keep themselves to themselves and to be rather shy and retiring will find that if they do make the effort to go out more, their social life will improve substantially and the year will prove one of the happiest and most enjoyable that they have had for a long time.

Naturally no year is without its problems, but any problems that do arise are likely to be minor and can be quickly dealt with. The one area that the Snake does need to watch, however, is if he has a difference of opinion with someone or arouses any jealousy in a colleague or friend. If such a situation arises, the Snake would do well to deal with the root cause. He could find that by tackling problems directly in his own inimitable way, he will win the admiration and respect of those around him and will go a long way towards solving the problem.

The year will prove quite busy for the Snake and it is important that he regularly sets some time aside for recreational pursuits. Also, if he is not able to get much exercise during the day, he will find some regular and suitable exercise such as walking, swimming or some sporting activity will do much to improve his well-being.

Although most Snakes will not travel too far over the year, the journeys the Snake does undertake will work out well, and he will thoroughly enjoy any holidays and short breaks.

Generally, 1993 will be a highly favourable year for the Snake. However it is up to him to persevere and go after the opportunities he sees. By acting positively and decisively, the Snake will be able to make tremendous progress and reap the rewards which perhaps have been eluding him in recent years.

As far as the different types of Snake are concerned, 1993 will be a most positive and fulfilling year for the **Metal Snake**. He is likely to make significant progress in his work and many Metal Snakes can look forward to promotion or to obtaining a new and more challenging position. The Metal Snake should keep alert for opportunities to pursue and even if he meets with initial set-backs, he should keep persevering. The gains he can make over the year can be quite considerable. The Metal Snake does, however, have a tendency to keep his plans and ideas to himself, and it would certainly be in his interests to be more open and to involve others in his activities. Those around him want to see him succeed but, in order to help him, they do need to know what he himself desires. The Metal Snake will be fortunate in financial matters over the year and if he does have any spare funds to invest, he will find that a long-term savings policy or an investment made with an eye to the future will prove an important asset in years to come. He will also be lucky in some purchases that he makes and by keeping alert he may find some bargains in the most unlikely of places. The Metal Snake will have some very happy times with his family and friends over the year and will lead a pleasant and active social life. He will also derive much satisfaction from his various interests and hobbies over the year – especially if they provide him with a complete change from his usual daytime activities.

This will be an important and highly significant year for the **Water Snake**. His patience and past efforts are now likely to be rewarded and he can make spectacular progress over the year. He should promote his work and skills as much as he can and should pursue any opportunities he sees. His gains over the year can be truly tremendous, but to make the most of these auspicious trends, the Water Snake must be bold and assertive. Sometimes he is not always as forthcoming as he should be, and in 1993 he should try to overcome any reticence that he has and make the most of his abilities. The progress which he makes over the year will not only be substantial but will have an important bearing on succeeding years as well – so much so, that many Water Snakes will come to look back on 1993 as one of the major turning points in their life. The Water Snake's home life will be busy and enjoyable over the year. His family and friends will be most supportive and if, at any time in the year, he needs advice or is in a dilemma, he will be considerably helped by the guidance and assistance that those around him can give. In view of the many demands on the Water Snake over the year, it is essential that he does not drive himself relentlessly but allows himself time to regularly unwind and rest. If not, he could fall victim to stress and tension and this could easily mar what will otherwise be an excellent year for him.

This will be a year of change for the **Wood Snake**. Many will take on new responsibilities in their work or obtain a different and more challenging position. Indeed, anything that the Wood Snake can do to broaden his experience or increase his skills will not only serve him well now, but in the next few years as well. The Wood Snake should follow up any opportunities that he sees and, with a determined and concerted effort, he will make pleasing progress. Some Wood Snakes will also change their accommodation over the year and while this will be unsettling at the time, they will find that the move will work out well for them. The Wood Snake will be reasonably successful in financial matters over the year, although he does still need to watch his general level of expenditure with care. He can also look forward to having some splendid times with his family and friends and a younger relation in particular is likely to be a great source of joy to him. The Wood Snake is often quite gifted in the arts and if he is able to spend time over the year in a creative activity, he will find that this will prove most satisfying for him and be an excellent outlet for his talents. Likewise, if he has been thinking of taking up a craft or a new interest, then this would be an ideal year to do so.

This will be an enjoyable and successful year for the **Fire Snake**. He will lead an active and pleasant social life and will make some very good friends as the year progresses. He will also be helped a considerable amount over the year by his family. However, although he will find that those around him are generally supportive in his various activities, he would do well to listen to any advice he is given, particularly concerning his future. Although he may not at first agree with all he is told, the advice will be given with his best interests at heart and there will be much wisdom in it. This will also be a very good year for the Fire Snake academically and, by applying himself and concentrating on specific objectives, he can make excellent progress. Also, if he is able to further his skills in any way, he will find this will do much to enhance his prospects in both this and future years. He will derive much pleasure from his hobbies and interests in 1993, particularly from any that allow him to meet others or involve him in outdoor activities. Travel is also favourably aspected.

This will be a good and generally pleasant year for the **Earth Snake**. His domestic life in particular will give him much pleasure and he can look forward to having some most enjoyable times with his family and friends. He will also have cause for a family celebration in 1993 as well as having the opportunity of seeing some close friends he has not seen for some considerable while. He will also be able to devote time to his various interests over the year and these are likely to be a great source of pleasure for him. He will do well in business and financial matters and many Earth Snakes can look forward to receiving a sum of money from the fruition of an investment or from some service they have done in the past. Many Earth Snakes will also spend some of their time over the year in DIY projects around their home and garden and, while they will be pleased with the finished result, the Earth Snake should nevertheless be careful not to strain himself when moving heavy objects or take unnecessary risks when using dangerous pieces of equipment. He also needs to exercise care with any important forms or pieces of correspondence he receives and should be fully aware of all the implications involved before signing any agreement. If in doubt, he would do well to seek professional advice. The Earth Snake will also have several strokes of luck over the year and could be successful in a competition that he enters in the first half of the year.

Famous Snakes

Muhammad Ali, Ann-Margret, Paddy Ashdown, Ronnie Barker, Kim Basinger, William Blake, Brahms, Raymond Burr, Dick Cheney, Julie Christie, Len Deighton, Fats Domino, Bob Dylan, Stefan Edberg, Elgar, Mahatma Gandhi, Greta Garbo, J. Paul Getty, W.E. Gladstone, Graham Gooch, Princess Grace of Monaco, Linda Gray, Bob Hawke, Nigel Hawthorne, Denis Healey, Paul Hogan, Howard Hughes, Rev. Jesse Jackson, Derek Jameson, Griff Rhys Jones, Gorden Kaye, J.F. Kennedy, Carole King, Abraham Lincoln, Dame Vera Lynn, Craig McLachlan, Magnus Magnusson, Mao Tse-tung, Nigel Mansell, Dean Martin, Henri Matisse, Robert Mitchum, Nasser, Bob Newhart, Aristotle Onassis, Jacqueline Onassis, Ryan O'Neal, Pablo Picasso, Edgar Allan Poe, André Previn, Brian Redhead, Jean-Paul Sartre, Franz Schubert, Brooke Shields, Paul Simon, Delia Smith, John Thaw, Tina Turner, Oprah Winfrey, Victoria Wood, Virginia Woolf, Mike Yarwood, Susannah York.

The Horse

25 January 1906	to	12 February 1907	*Fire Horse*
11 February 1918	to	31 January 1919	*Earth Horse*
30 January 1930	to	16 February 1931	*Metal Horse*
15 February 1942	to	4 February 1943	*Water Horse*
3 February 1954	to	23 January 1955	*Wood Horse*
21 January 1966	to	8 February 1967	*Fire Horse*
7 February 1978	to	27 January 1979	*Earth Horse*
27 January 1990	to	14 February 1991	*Metal Horse*

The Personality of the Horse

It is only through labor and painful effort, by grim energy and resolute courage that we move on to better things.
– *Theodore Roosevelt: a Horse.*

The Horse is born under the signs of elegance and ardour. He has a most engaging and charming manner and is usually very popular. He loves meeting people and likes attending parties and other large social gatherings.

He is a lively character and enjoys being the centre of attention. He has considerable leadership qualities and is much admired for his honest and straightforward manner. He is an eloquent and persuasive speaker and has a great love of discussion and debate. The Horse also has a particularly agile mind and can assimilate facts remarkably quickly.

He does, however, have a fiery temper and although his outbursts are usually short-lived, he can often say things which he will later regret. He is also not particularly good at keeping secrets.

The Horse has many interests and involves himself in a wide variety of activities. He can, however, get involved in so much that he can often waste his energies on projects which he never has time to complete. He also has a tendency to change his interests rather frequently and will often get caught up with the latest craze or 'in thing' until something better or more exciting turns up.

The Horse also likes to have a certain amount of freedom and independence in the things that he does. He hates being bound by petty rules and regulations and as far as possible he likes to feel that he is answerable to no one but himself. But despite this spirit of freedom, he still likes to have the support and encouragement of others in his various enterprises.

Due to his many talents and likeable nature, the Horse will often go far in life. He enjoys challenges and is a methodical and tireless worker. However, should things work against him and he fail with any of his enterprises, it will take a long time for him to recover and pick up the pieces again. Success to the Horse means everything. To fail is a disaster and a humiliation.

The Horse likes to have variety in his life and he will try his hand at many different things before he settles down to one particular job. Even then, he will probably remain alert to see if there are any new and better opportunities for him to take up. The Horse has a restless nature and can easily get bored. He does, however, excel in any position which allows him sufficient freedom to act on his own initiative or brings him into contact with a lot of people.

Although the Horse is not particularly bothered about accumulating great wealth, he handles his finances with care and will rarely experience any serious financial problems.

The Horse also enjoys travel and he loves visiting new and far-away places. At some stage during his life he will be tempted to live abroad for a short period of time and due to his adaptable nature he will find that he will fit in well wherever he goes.

The Horse pays a great deal of attention to his appearance and usually likes to wear smart, colourful and rather distinctive clothes. He is very attractive to the opposite sex and will often have many romances before he settles down. He is loyal and protective to his partner, but despite his family commitments he still likes to retain a certain measure of independence and have the freedom to carry on with his own interests and hobbies. He will find that he is especially well-suited to those born under the signs of the Tiger, Goat, Rooster and Dog. The Horse can also get on well with the Rabbit, Dragon, Snake, Pig and another Horse, but he will find the Ox too serious and intolerant for his liking. The Horse will also have difficulty in getting on with the Monkey and the Rat – the Monkey is very inquisitive and the Rat seeks security – and both will resent the Horse's rather independent ways.

The female Horse is usually most attractive and has a friendly, outgoing personality. She is highly intelligent, has many interests and is alert to everything that is going on around her. She particularly enjoys outdoor pursuits and often likes to take part in sport and keep-fit activities. She also enjoys travel, literature and the arts, and is a very good conversationalist.

Although the Horse can be stubborn and rather self-centred, he does have a considerate nature and is often willing to help others. He has a good sense of humour and will usually make a favourable impression wherever he goes. Provided he can curb his slightly restless nature and keep a tight control over his temper, the Horse will go through life making friends, taking part in a multitude of different activities and generally achieving many of his objectives. His life will rarely be dull.

The Five Different Types of Horse

In addition to the 12 signs of the Chinese zodiac, there are five elements, and these have a strengthening or moderating influence on the sign. The effects of the five elements on the Horse are described below, together with the years in which the elements were exercising their influence. Therefore all Horses born in 1930 and 1990 are Metal Horses, those born in 1942 are Water Horses and so on.

Metal Horse: 1930, 1990
This Horse is bold, confident and forthright. He is ambitious and also a great innovator. He loves challenges and takes great delight in sorting out complicated problems. He likes to have a certain amount of independence in the things that he does and resents any outside interference. The Metal Horse has charm and a certain charisma, but he can also be very stubborn and rather impulsive. He usually has many friends and enjoys an active social life.

Water Horse: 1942
The Water Horse has a friendly nature, a good sense of humour, and is able to talk intelligently on a wide range of topics. He is astute in business matters and is quick to take advantage of any opportunities that arise. He does, however, have a tendency to get easily distracted and can change his interests – and indeed his mind – rather frequently, and this can often work to his detriment. He is nevertheless very talented and can often go far in life. He pays a great deal of attention to his appearance and is usually smart and well turned out. He loves to travel and also enjoys sport and other outdoor activities.

Wood Horse: 1894, 1954
The Wood Horse has a most agreeable and amiable nature. He communicates well with others and, like the Water

Horse, is able to talk intelligently on many different subjects. He is a hard and conscientious worker and is held in high esteem by his friends and colleagues. His opinions and views are often sought and, given his imaginative nature, he can quite often come up with some very original and practical ideas. He is usually widely read and likes to lead a busy social life. He can also be most generous and often holds high moral viewpoints.

Fire Horse: 1906, 1966
The element of Fire combined with the temperament of the Horse creates one of the most powerful forces in the Chinese zodiac. The Fire Horse is destined to lead an exciting and eventful life and to make his mark in his chosen profession. He has a forceful personality and his intelligence and resolute manner bring him the support and admiration of many. He loves action and excitement and his life will rarely be quiet. He can, however, be rather blunt and forthright in his views and does not take kindly to interference in his own affairs or to obeying orders. He is a flamboyant character, has a good sense of humour, and will lead a very active social life.

Earth Horse: 1918, 1978
This Horse is considerate and caring. He is more cautious than some of the other types of Horse, but he is wise, perceptive and extremely capable. Although he can be rather indecisive at times, he has considerable business acumen and is very astute in financial matters. He has a quiet, friendly nature and is well thought of by his family and friends.

Prospects for the Horse in 1993

The Chinese New Year starts on 23 January 1993. Until then, the old year, the year of the Monkey, is still making its presence felt.

The year of the Monkey (4 February 1992 to 22 January 1993) is likely to have been a generally favourable year for the Horse. He will have made satisfying progress in many of his activities and will have gained some valuable experience over the year, experience which will serve him well in the future.

The closing stages of the Monkey year can be a most constructive time for the Horse. He should pursue any opportunities that he sees, particularly as far as his work interests are concerned, and should promote his many skills and talents. Any Horse who is seeking employment, wanting to change his position or looking for promotion could find his efforts rewarded at this time.

The Horse will also lead a most pleasant social life at this time and is likely to attend some enjoyable functions. Domestic matters are particularly well aspected and the Horse can look forward to having some memorable times with his family and friends over the Christmas and New Year holidays.

On a more cautionary note, however, the Horse does need to exercise care in financial matters at the end of the Monkey year and would do well not to get involved in any risky enterprises or stretch his resources too far. Provided he is careful in financial matters and continues to set about his activities in his own conscientious manner, he will emerge from the year with many worthwhile gains to his credit. He will be able to put these to good use in the year ahead.

The year of the Rooster begins on 23 January 1993 and is going to be a busy and fulfilling year for the Horse. He will be able to make progress in many of his activities, but it will be a year in which he will need to work hard in order to secure the results he desires.

The area in which the Horse could experience most problems is in his relations with others. These problems are not likely to be serious but could principally arise out of a clash of personalities or a difference of opinion. When such a situation does arise, the Horse should try to deal with the problem as quickly and as amicably as he can. If not, any souring of relations could hamper his progress and spoil what could otherwise be a good year for him. The Horse should also watch his temper over the year, and should he find himself in any contentious discussion, he would do well to exercise restraint over what he says. This is very much a year in which the Horse needs to be tactful and discreet.

However, despite this need for care in the handling of relations, the year will hold many happy moments for the Horse. Domestically, this will be a most pleasant year for him, and his family and friends will be particularly supportive and encouraging in their attitude. In return, the Horse should make every effort to involve those around him in his activities. His home life throughout the Rooster year will be most settled and content – providing he can keep a close watch over that rather forthright tongue of his! Although there will be numerous demands on their time over the year, many Horses will carry out alterations to their home or garden, and the work that they do will give them much pleasure and satisfaction.

Travel is also favourably aspected and the Horse can look forward to undertaking several interesting journeys over the year. He will also find local outings or short breaks especially enjoyable.

The Horse will be reasonably fortunate in financial matters in 1993. However, if he is able to carry out a review of his general outgoings and financial position, he will notice that a few modifications will make a considerable difference. The Horse is also likely to make some large purchases for his home – notably pieces of household equipment – and by looking around, he will obtain several items at most favourable prices.

In his work, the Horse will continue to make progress. There are indications that many Horses will change their position over the year and be successful in obtaining new and more challenging work. However, at all times, the Horse will need to remain vigilant and cannot afford to take things for granted. To achieve success in 1993, the Horse will need to assert himself and work hard. He will also need to remain aware of the views of his colleagues and avoid acting independently or without the support of others. As has been mentioned, throughout 1993 the Horse does need to take great care over how he handles his relations with others and this particularly applies to his colleagues and those around him. Throughout the year he would do well to remember the Chinese proverb 'Patience in a moment of anger will spare you a hundred days of anguish.'

In the year of the Rooster the Horse will lead a quiet but pleasant social life. There will be opportunities for him to build up some new and long-lasting friendships and some of these could prove of considerable importance to his future progress, particularly next year, the year of the Dog.

Generally, this will be a pleasing and enjoyable year for the Horse. He can look forward to making good and steady progress in most of his activities, although to get the results he desires he will need to apply himself and work hard. However, the Horse is well noted for his diligence and ability for hard work and by continuing to set about his activities in a positive and conscientious manner, he will do well over the year.

As far as the different types of Horse are concerned, this will be an interesting and varied year for the **Metal Horse**. He will be able to devote considerable time to his hobbies and interests and these are likely to be a great source of pleasure for him. There will also be several opportunities to travel in 1993 and the journeys that he does undertake will prove especially enjoyable. Domestically, this will also be a good year and the Metal Horse will take particular delight in the achievements of someone close to him. However, despite these generally good trends, the year can all too easily be spoilt. The Metal Horse does have a stubborn streak in him and if he finds himself in an

awkward situation or has a conflict of opinion with
someone, he could find an intransigent or stubborn attitude
will lead to a worsening of the situation and bring him more
problems. In 1993 the Metal Horse does need to handle his
relations with others with care and deal with any problems
in a reasonable manner. Failure to do so could mar what
will otherwise be a good year for him, as well as taking up
time which he could spend on more pleasurable activities.
Hopefully, any differences or problems that arise will be
relatively minor ones, but to get best results over the year,
the Metal Horse would do well to heed this advice.

This will be an interesting but challenging year for the
Water Horse. To make any progress, however, he will
need to work hard and concentrate on specific objectives.
To try and undertake too many things or commit himself
to more activities than he can sensibly handle at any one
time will only limit his progress and lead to less satisfying
results. As far as possible, the Water Horse should draw
up a set of priorities for the year and concentrate on those
activities that he knows he has time to complete and deal
with satisfactorily. This particularly applies to his work
and his career. Progress and advancement is possible, but
only with much application on his part. The Water Horse
will also face several problems or obstacles over the year
and, while not serious, he would do well to deal with the
problems decisively and as effectively as he can. Should
events at any time in the year go against him, he should
regard what has happened as a new opportunity and a
challenge which he can, with determination, assuredly
triumph over. The Water Horse will, however, be
successful in financial matters in 1993 and an investment
or a savings policy that he takes out could prove an
excellent asset in years to come. He can also look forward
to some happy times with his family and friends over the
year and any projects that he carries out on his home will
prove both satisfying and rewarding. Travel is also well
aspected and many Water Horses will go on some

interesting and illuminating journeys in 1993.

This will be a generally pleasant year for the **Wood Horse**. He can look forward to making progress in his work and will be generally pleased with his accomplishments. He may, however, find that some of his plans have to be altered or that he has to adapt to new situations, but providing he is prepared to be flexible and accommodating in his outlook, he could find that the changes that take place (particularly in his work) will work out well and will be very much to his long-term advantage. Throughout the year, the Wood Horse needs to keep a close watch on all that is going on around him and make sure that he keeps those close to him fully informed of his views and feelings. Failure to do so could result in differences of opinion or tensions which, with care, could have been avoided. The Wood Horse will derive much satisfaction from his various interests over the year, especially from any that involve him in creative or outdoor pursuits. He will also enjoy the travelling that he undertakes over the year. Financial matters are generally well aspected, although it would be in the Wood Horse's interests to keep a watchful eye over his general level of expenditure.

This will be a year of change for the **Fire Horse**, and the changes could concern almost any aspect of his life. For some it could be a personal celebration, such as getting married or having an addition to his family, for others it could be a change in accommodation or a change in work. The changes that do take place will prove very positive for the Fire Horse, however, and in some respects will mark a significant upturn in his fortunes. Indeed, the Fire Horse can do extremely well over the year and will make considerable progress in many of his activities. But in order to maximize these good trends, the Fire Horse should have some clear idea in his mind of what he wants to achieve over the year and also be willing to discuss his plans and ideas with others. Sometimes he can be guilty of trying to do too much on his own or of retaining too much of an independent attitude and this is something he would do well to try and curb in the year of the Rooster. For the best results, he needs to work closely with others. The Fire Horse will also have some luck in money matters over the year, and many can look forward to an improvement in their financial situation. Domestically and socially, this will be a very fulfilling and enjoyable year.

This will prove a particularly significant year for the **Earth Horse**. Over the course of the year he is likely to give much thought to his future but, before arriving at any firm decision, he would do well to seek the advice and opinions of those around him. Provided he acts carefully and in his usual level-headed manner, any decisions that he makes will work out well for him. Academically, this will also be a good year for the Earth Horse and as long as he is prepared to work hard and concentrate on specific objectives he will do well. The main danger is if he tries to do too much in too short a time or gets distracted by less important matters. However, if he is persistent and exercises a certain amount of self-discipline, his progress over the year will be most rewarding and particularly beneficial to his future. The Earth Horse will lead an active social life and can look forward to attending several enjoyable parties and functions over the year. Although the year will be a generally good one for the Earth Horse, if he does experience any set-backs or reversals to his plans he should adopt a positive tone, learn from any mistakes he has made, and keep his eye firmly fixed on the future. Persistence and confidence will bring its rewards.

Famous Horses

Neil Armstrong, Rowan Atkinson, Cheryl Baker, James Baker, King Baudouin of Belgium, Samuel Beckett, Leonard Bernstein, Sir John Betjeman, Karen Black, Gayle Blakeney, Gillian Blakeney, Nicholas Brady, Leonid Brezhnev, Ray

Charles, Chopin, Sean Connery, Billy Connolly, Catherine Cookson, Ronnie Corbett, Elvis Costello, Kevin Costner, Jim Davidson, Anne Diamond, Clint Eastwood, Thomas Alva Edison, Linda Evans, Chris Evert, Harrison Ford, Aretha Franklin, Bob Geldof, Billy Graham, Larry Grayson, Gene Hackman, Rolf Harris, Ted Hughes, Douglas Hurd, Janet Jackson, Gerald Kaufman, Nikita Khrushchev, Robert Kilroy-Silk, Neil Kinnock, Dr Helmut Kohl, Eddie Large, Lenin, Annie Lennox, Syd Little, Desmond Lynam, Paul McCartney, Harold Macmillan, Nelson Mandela, Princess Margaret, Spike Milligan, Ben Murphy, Sir Isaac Newton, Louis Pasteur, Harold Pinter, J.B. Priestley, Puccini, Claire Rayner, Rembrandt, Ruth Rendell, Franklin D. Roosevelt, Anwar Sadat, Peter Sissons, Lord Snowdon, Alexander Solzhenitsyn, Lisa Stansfield, Barbra Streisand, John Travolta, Freddie Trueman, Mike Tyson, Vivaldi, Lord Whitelaw, Andy Williams, the Duke of Windsor, Tammy Wynette, Boris Yeltsin, Michael York.

ΤΡΑΓΕΔΟΙ

The Goat

13 February 1907 to	1 February 1908	*Fire Goat*
1 February 1919 to	19 February 1920	*Earth Goat*
17 February 1931 to	5 February 1932	*Metal Goat*
5 February 1943 to	24 January 1944	*Water Goat*
24 January 1955 to	11 February 1956	*Wood Goat*
9 February 1967 to	29 January 1968	*Fire Goat*
28 January 1979 to	15 February 1980	*Earth Goat*
15 February 1991 to	3 February 1992	*Metal Goat*

The Personality of the Goat

Always do right; this will gratify some people and
astonish the rest.
– *Mark Twain: a Goat.*

The Goat is born under the sign of art. He is imaginative,
creative and has a good appreciation of the finer things in
life. He has an easy-going nature and prefers to live in a
relaxed and pressure-free environment. He hates any sort
of discord or unpleasantness and does not like to be bound
by a strict routine or rigid timetable. The Goat is not one
to be hurried against his will but, despite his seemingly
relaxed approach to life, he is something of a perfectionist
and when he starts work on a project he is certain to give
of his best.

The Goat usually prefers to work in a team rather than
on his own. He likes to have the support and encourage-

ment of others and if left to deal with matters on his own he can get very worried and tends to view things rather pessimistically. Wherever possible the Goat will leave major decision-making to others while he concentrates on his own pursuits. If, however, he feels particularly strongly about a certain matter or has to defend his position in any way, he will act with great fortitude and precision.

The Goat has a very persuasive nature and often uses his considerable charm to get his own way. He can, however, be rather hesitant about letting his true feelings be known and if he were prepared to be more forthright he would do much better as a result.

The Goat tends to have a quiet, somewhat reserved nature but when he is in company that he likes he can often become the centre of attention. He can be highly amusing, a marvellous host at parties, and a superb entertainer. Whenever the spotlight falls on the Goat, his adrenalin starts to flow and he can be assured of giving a sparkling performance – particularly if he is allowed to use his creative skills in any way.

Of all the signs in the Chinese zodiac, the Goat is probably the most gifted artistically. Whether it is in the theatre, literature, music or art, the Goat is certain to make a lasting impression. He is a born creator and is rarely happier than when occupied in some artistic pursuit. But even in this, the Goat does well to work with others rather than on his own. He needs inspiration and a guiding influence, but when he has found his true *métier*, he can often receive widespread acclaim and recognition.

In addition to his liking for the arts, the Goat is usually quite religious and often has a deep interest in nature, animals and the countryside. The Goat is also fairly athletic and there are many who have excelled in some form of sporting activity.

Although the Goat is not particularly materialistic or concerned about finance, he will find that he will usually be lucky in financial matters and will rarely be short of the necessary funds to tide himself over. He is, however, rather indulgent and tends to spend his money as soon as he receives it rather than make provision for the future.

The Goat usually leaves home when he is young but he will always maintain strong links with his parents and the other members of his family. He is also rather nostalgic and is well known for keeping mementoes of his childhood and souvenirs of places that he has visited. His home will not be particularly tidy but he knows where everything is and it will also be scrupulously clean.

Affairs of the heart are particularly important to the Goat and he will often have many romances before he finally settles down. Although the Goat is fairly adaptable, he prefers to live in a secure and stable environment and he will find that he is best suited to those born under the signs of the Tiger, Horse, Monkey, Pig and Rabbit. He can also establish a good relationship with the Dragon, Snake, Rooster and another Goat, but he may find the Ox and Dog a little too serious for his liking. Neither will he care particularly for the Rat's rather thrifty ways.

The lady Goat devotes all her time and energy to the needs of her family. She has excellent taste in home furnishings and often uses her considerable artistic skills to make clothes for herself and her children. She takes great care over her appearance and can be most attractive to the opposite sex. Although she is not the most well-organized of people, her engaging manner and delightful sense of humour creates a favourable impression wherever she goes. She is also a good cook and usually gets much pleasure from gardening and outdoor pursuits.

The Goat can win friends easily and people generally feel relaxed in his company. He has a kind and understanding nature and although he can occasionally be stubborn, he can, with the right support and encouragement, live a happy and very satisfying life. The more he can use his creative skills, the happier he will be.

The Five Different Types of Goat

In addition to the 12 signs of the Chinese zodiac, there are five elements, and these have a strengthening or moderating influence on the sign. The effects of the five elements on the Goat are described below, together with the years in which the elements were exercising their influence. Therefore all Goats born in 1931 and 1991 are Metal Goats, those born in 1943 are Water Goats, and so on.

Metal Goat: 1931, 1991
This Goat is thorough and conscientious in all that he does and is capable of doing very well in his chosen profession. Despite his confident manner, he can be a great worrier and he would find it a help if he were more prepared to discuss his worries with others rather than keep them to himself. He is loyal to his family and employers and will have a small group of extremely good friends. He has good artistic taste and is usually highly skilled in some aspect of the arts. He is often a collector of antiques and his home will be very tastefully furnished.

Water Goat: 1943
The Water Goat is very popular and makes friends with remarkable ease. He is good at spotting opportunities but does not always have the necessary confidence to follow them through. He likes to have security both in his home life and at work and does not take kindly to change. He is articulate, has a good sense of humour, and is usually very good with children.

Wood Goat: 1895, 1955
This Goat is generous, kind-hearted and always eager to please. He usually has a large circle of friends and involves himself in a wide variety of different activities. He has a very trusting nature but he can sometimes give in to the demands of others a little too easily and it would be in his

own interests if he were to stand his ground a little more often. He is usually lucky in financial matters and, like the Water Goat, is very good with children.

Fire Goat: 1907, 1967

This Goat usually knows what he wants in life and he often uses his considerable charm and persuasive personality in order to achieve his aims. He can sometimes let his imagination run away with him and has a tendency to ignore matters which are not to his liking. He is rather extravagant in his spending and would do well to exercise a little more care when dealing with financial matters. He has a lively personality, has many friends, and loves attending parties and social occasions.

Earth Goat: 1919, 1979

This Goat has a very considerate and caring nature. He is particularly loyal to his family and friends and invariably creates a favourable impression wherever he goes. He is reliable and conscientious in his work but he finds it difficult to save and never likes to deprive himself of any little luxury which he might fancy. He has numerous interests and is often very well read. He usually gets much pleasure from following the activities of various members of his family.

Prospects for the Goat in 1993

The Chinese New Year starts on 23 January 1993. Until then, the old year, the year of the Monkey, is still making its presence felt.

The year of the Monkey (4 February 1992 to 22 January 1993) is likely to have been a relatively busy year for the Goat and, although not all the events of the year may have been to his liking, he will still have achieved a considerable amount.

The Goat will have impressed others over the year and this, together with the experience he has gained, will serve him well for the future. He is also likely to have made progress in his work and this will put him in a good position to make further advances in the year ahead. Those Goats seeking work should remain alert for opportunities and for ways in which they can use their skills. Also, if they are able to talk to those who may be in a position to offer assistance, Goats could be given some advice which will prove of great importance in the year ahead. The latter part of the Monkey year and early part of the Rooster year can be a very important time for all Goats, and the events that occur and advice they are given could prove of more significance than they may realize at the time.

Socially, the closing stages of the year will be a busy period for the Goat and he can look forward to some most enjoyable times with his family and friends. There will, however, be some Goats who have experienced difficulties and tensions in their relations with others over the year. For these Goats, the closing weeks of the year will give them an ideal time to sort out any differences and disagreements that might still remain. All Goats would also do well to take advantage of any opportunity that they get to relax and unwind over the Christmas and New Year break. The strains, pressures and activities of the year will have taken a lot out of them. Refreshed and revitalized, the Goat will be better able to take advantage of the favourable trends that lie ahead.

The year of the Rooster starts on 23 January 1993 and is going to be an interesting and varied year for the Goat.

Many Goats, in the last few years, may have become dissatisfied with their present position and want a change. This can apply to where they live, to their work, or to some other area of their life. In 1993, the changes will begin to take place and many Goats will notice a subtle upturn in their fortunes. This upturn will not be immediate or dramatic, but will take place over the course of the year.

The Goat will find that his hopes and plans are at last becoming realized and that he is making the progress he has long desired.

If the Goat wants to move house, this will be an ideal year to do so. Although the move could prove time-consuming and involve the Goat in some anxious moments, the end result will be very pleasing to him. He could also feel refreshed and stimulated by a change in his environment and be pleased to have the opportunity to make new friends and live in a new area.

If the Goat is wanting to change his type of work, seeking promotion or looking for employment, he should follow up the opportunities that he will see over the year. He would also do well to try and broaden his skills and qualifications, and if there are any courses that he can go on or is any way he can extend his knowledge, he will find this will do much to enhance his prospects.

Progress, in almost any sphere of the Goat's life, is possible in the year of the Rooster, but much does depend on the Goat's own attitude and degree of determination. Provided he has an objective or goal in mind and sets about achieving this in a determined and methodical way, the Goat will do well and benefit from the generally favourable trends that prevail.

The Goat will lead an active and enjoyable social life over the year and will also derive much pleasure from his interests and recreational activities. Outdoor pursuits and travel are particularly well aspected, and for those Goats who have thought about undertaking a long journey or working in another country, 1993 would be an excellent year to do so.

Naturally no year is without its problems and there are certain areas that the Goat will need to watch. One of these is finance. This will be a generally expensive year for the Goat and while he may himself recognize that he is spending a great deal of money – particularly if he is changing his accommodation, having home improvements carried out or travelling – it would be very much in his interest to keep a close watch on his level of expenditure. If he is about to enter into a large transaction he should try to obtain several quotations before he proceeds and also make sure that he is conversant with all the terms of the transaction. Providing he is careful and prudent, the Goat could save himself unnecessary expense and avoid possible problems later.

The other area that could pose problems for the Goat is his relations with others. Occasionally the Goat can be reticent about expressing his views and feelings and this can give rise to misunderstandings and possible friction. In the year of the Rooster, the Goat should try to be more open and forthright and not be hesitant about expressing his true views. He would also do well to seek the advice and opinions of others over the year – particularly on any matter that might be giving him cause for concern. The Goat will find those around him supportive and willing to help.

Generally, 1993 will be a pleasing year for the Goat. It will hold many enjoyable and satisfying moments for him and the changes that take place over the year are likely to be of lasting benefit. In 1993 the Goat should act positively and determinedly, and providing he does so, he will do well and sow the seeds for future progress.

As far as the different types of Goat are concerned, 1993 will be a generally satisfying year for the **Metal Goat**. Social activities will go well and he will be much in demand with his family and friends. He can also look forward to taking part in a major family celebration as well as attending some most enjoyable social functions. Travel is well aspected and the journeys that he goes on are likely to prove most interesting, especially if he visits areas that are unfamiliar to him. The Metal Goat will be relatively successful in business and work matters in 1993. However, in all that he does, he cannot afford to be complacent. He should set about his various undertakings with care and in his usual diligent way. He will also need to exercise much patience over the year for, although his accomplishments will be substantial, the results that he wants may not always be as immediate or as forthcoming as he may desire. The Metal Goat will also obtain considerable pleasure from creative and outdoor pursuits and any Metal Goat who changes his accommodation in 1993 will find that this will work out well for him.

This will be an important year for the **Water Goat**. Over the course of the year he will see several opportunities which will allow him to improve his position and providing he acts determinedly and decisively, he can do extremely well, especially as far as his career is concerned. He would also do well to give some thought to his future and draw up some objectives to aim for. Without this, the Water Goat could let some opportunities pass by and not reap the success that he could otherwise obtain. He should also make every effort to involve his family and friends in his various activities and seek their opinion on any problem that may be troubling him or about any important decision he has to take. He will be considerably gratified by the advice and assistance he is given. The Water Goat will lead a pleasant family and social life over the year and while he may not always have as much time to devote to his hobbies and interests as he would like, he should make sure that he does set some regular time aside for recreational activities and allow himself the opportunity to unwind from his usual routine. Without this, the Water Goat could fall victim to stress and tension and feel below par. It would also be in his interests to exercise great care in financial matters and keep a close watch on his general level of spending. A few modifications to his regular outgoings could make a surprising difference.

This will be a quiet but generally enjoyable year for the **Wood Goat**. He will make steady progress in most of his activities and in his work he could be given some new, interesting and challenging responsibilities. The Wood

Goat will impress many around him with his caring and attentive attitude and this will help his prospects, particularly in the second half of the year. The Wood Goat will also lead a content domestic life over the year and be much in demand with his family and friends. A younger relation in particular is likely to be a great source of pride to him over the year. The Wood Goat will, however, need to watch his general level of spending in 1993 and would do well not to stretch his resources too far. He also needs to deal with any official or important correspondence that he receives carefully and promptly – a delay could be to his detriment. Those Wood Goats who are not able to take much exercise during the day would do well to consider taking up some suitable exercise course or sporting activity. They will find that this will do much to improve their well-being. Travel is well aspected over the year and a holiday or break taken at short notice could prove especially enjoyable.

This will be an interesting and potentially rewarding year for the **Fire Goat**. He can look forward to having some most enjoyable times with his family and friends, and socially and domestically this will be a busy and happy year for him. Also, many Fire Goats will see an addition to their family over the year. The Fire Goat is likely to do well in his work although the amount of progress he makes is very much in his own hands. Although the Fire Goat usually has a clear idea of what he wants to achieve in the long run, he can sometimes be guilty of setting himself unrealistic short-term objectives or of being over-ambitious. In 1993 he would do well to draw up a set of priorities and objectives for the year and to pursue these in his own determined and inimitable way. This year he should plan then act, for without any plan he could miss some excellent opportunities that could be to his advantage. On a cautionary note, the Fire Goat would do well to watch his general level of spending over the year.

This will be a generally quiet but pleasant year for the

Earth Goat. He can look forward to having some most enjoyable times with his family and friends as well as leading an active social life. Any Earth Goat who may have felt lonely in recent years or who has some spare time at his disposal should certainly make every effort to go out more, join a local society or take up a new interest. This is a year for acting positively and providing he does, the Earth Goat will notice an upturn in his social life and find this a more enjoyable and satisfying year than recent years may have been. Travel is also well aspected and the holidays and journeys that the Earth Goat takes will prove particularly enjoyable and could lead to several new friendships. Those Earth Goats in education are also likely to make pleasing progress. The Earth Goat does particularly value his relations with others and if he finds himself involved in a difference of opinion with anyone, he would do well to deal with the problem as quickly and as effectively as he can. To let any strain in a personal relationship linger could cause the Earth Goat unnecessary anguish and mar what will otherwise be a good year for him.

Famous Goats

Dame Peggy Ashcroft, Isaac Asimov, Jane Austen, Boris Becker, Ian Botham, John le Carré, Nat 'King' Cole, Catherine Deneuve, John Denver, Arthur Conan Doyle, Douglas Fairbanks, Dame Margot Fonteyn, Anna Ford, Paul Gascoigne, Paul Michael Glaser, Sharon Gless, Mikhail Gorbachev, Larry Hagman, George Harrison, Sir Edmund Hillary, Julio Iglesias, Mick Jagger, Ben Kingsley, David Kossoff, Doris Lessing, Peter Lilley, Franz Liszt, John Major, Michelangelo, Cliff Michelmore, Joni Mitchell, Edwin Moses, Frank Muir, Rupert Murdoch, Mussolini, Leonard Nimoy, Robert de Niro, Des O'Connor, Lord Olivier, Michael Palin, Cecil Parkinson, Javier Perez de Cuellar,

Alain Prost, Keith Richards, Sir Malcolm Sargent, Mike Smith, Freddie Starr, Norman Tebbit, Leslie Thomas, Mark Twain, Rudolph Valentino, Vangelis, Lech Walesa, Barbara Walters, Andy Warhol, John Wayne, Bruce Willis, Debra Winger, Paul Young.

The Monkey

2 February 1908 to	21 January 1909	*Earth Monkey*
20 February 1920 to	7 February 1921	*Metal Monkey*
6 February 1932 to	25 January 1933	*Water Monkey*
25 January 1944 to	12 February 1945	*Wood Monkey*
12 February 1956 to	30 January 1957	*Fire Monkey*
30 January 1968 to	16 February 1969	*Earth Monkey*
16 February 1980 to	4 February 1981	*Metal Monkey*
4 February 1992 to	22 January 1993	*Water Monkey*

The Personality of the Monkey

Life was meant to be lived, and curiosity must be kept
alive. One must never, for whatever reason, turn his
back on life.
                              – *Eleanor Roosevelt: a Monkey.*

The Monkey is born under the sign of fantasy. He is
imaginative, inquisitive, and loves to keep an eye on
everything that is going on around him. He is never
backward in offering advice or trying to sort out the
problems of others. He likes to be helpful and his advice
is invariably sensible and reliable.

The Monkey is intelligent, well-read and always eager to
learn. He has an extremely good memory and there are
many Monkeys who have made particularly good linguists.
The Monkey is also a convincing talker and enjoys taking
part in discussions and debates. His friendly, self-assured

manner can be very persuasive and he usually has little trouble in winning people round to his way of thinking – it is for this reason that the Monkey often excels in politics and public speaking. He is also particularly adept in PR work, teaching and any job which involves selling.

The Monkey can, however, be crafty, cunning and occasionally dishonest, and he will seize on any opportunity to make a quick gain or outsmart his opponents. He has so much charm and guile that people often don't realize what he is up to until it is too late. But despite his resourceful nature, the Monkey does run the risk of outsmarting even himself. He has so much confidence in his abilities that he rarely listens to advice or is prepared to accept help from anyone. The Monkey likes to help others but prefers to rely on his own judgement when dealing with his own affairs.

Another characteristic of the Monkey is that he is extremely good at solving problems and has a happy knack of extricating himself (and others) from the most hopeless of positions. He is the master of self-preservation.

With so many diverse talents the Monkey is able to make considerable sums of money, but he does like to enjoy life and will think nothing of spending his money on some exotic holiday or luxury which he has had his eye on. He can, however, become very envious if someone else has got what he wants.

The Monkey is an original thinker and, despite his love of company, he cherishes his independence. He has to have the freedom to act as he wants and any Monkey who feels hemmed in or bound by too many restrictions can soon become unhappy. Likewise, if anything becomes too boring or monotonous, he soon loses interest and turns his attention to something else. The Monkey lacks persistence and this can often hamper his progress. He is also easily distracted, a tendency which all Monkeys should try to overcome. The Monkey should concentrate on one thing at a time and by doing so will almost certainly achieve more in the long run.

The Monkey is a good organizer and, even though he may behave slightly erratically at times, he will invariably have some plan at the back of his mind. On the odd occasion when his plans do not quite work out, he is usually quite happy to shrug his shoulders and put it down to experience. He will rarely make the same mistake twice and throughout his life he will try his hand at many things.

The Monkey likes to impress and is rarely without followers or admirers. There are many who are attracted to him by his good looks, his sense of humour, or simply because he instils so much confidence.

Monkeys usually marry young and for it to be a success their partner must allow them time to pursue their many interests and the opportunity to indulge in their love of travel. The Monkey has to have variety in his life and is especially well-suited to those born under the sociable and outgoing signs of the Rat, Dragon, Pig and Goat. The Ox, Rabbit, Snake and Dog will also be enchanted by the Monkey's resourceful and outgoing nature, but the Monkey is likely to exasperate the Rooster and Horse, and the Tiger will have little patience for the Monkey's tricks. A relationship between two Monkeys will also work well – they will understand each other and be able to assist each other in their various enterprises.

The lady Monkey is intelligent, extremely observant and a shrewd judge of character. Her opinions and views are often highly valued, and having such a persuasive nature, she invariably gets her own way. The lady Monkey has many interests and involves herself in a wide variety of activities. She pays great attention to her appearance, is an elegant dresser, and likes to take particular care over her hair. She can also be a most caring and doting parent and will have many good and loyal friends.

Provided the Monkey can curb his desire to take part in all that is going on around him and concentrate on one thing at a time, he can usually achieve what he wants in life. Should he suffer any disappointments, he is bound to bounce back. The Monkey is a survivor and his life is usually both colourful and very eventful.

The Five Different Types of Monkey

In addition to the 12 signs of the Chinese zodiac, there are five elements and these have a strengthening or moderating influence on the sign. The effects of the five elements on the Monkey are described below, together with the years in which the elements were exercising their influence. Therefore all Monkeys born in 1920 and 1980 are Metal Monkeys, those born in 1932 and 1992 are Water Monkeys, and so on.

Metal Monkey: 1920, 1980
The Metal Monkey is very strong-willed. He sets about everything he does with a dogged determination and often prefers to work independently rather than with others. He is ambitious, wise and confident, and is certainly not afraid of hard work. He is very astute in financial matters and usually chooses his investments well. Despite his somewhat independent nature, the Metal Monkey enjoys attending parties and social occasions and is particularly warm and caring towards his loved ones.

Water Monkey: 1932, 1992
The Water Monkey is versatile, determined and perceptive. He also has more discipline than some of the other Monkeys and is prepared to work towards a certain goal rather than be distracted by something else. He is not always open about his true intentions and when questioned can be particularly evasive. He can be sensitive to criticism but also very persuasive and usually has little trouble in getting others to fall in with his plans. He has a very good

understanding of human nature and relates well to others.

Wood Monkey: 1944

This Monkey is efficient, methodical and extremely conscientious. He is also highly imaginative and is always trying to capitalize on new ideas or learning new skills. Occasionally his enthusiasm can get the better of him and he can get very agitated when things do not quite work out as he had hoped. He does, however, have a very adventurous streak in him and is not afraid of taking risks. He also loves travel. He is usually held in great esteem by his friends and colleagues.

Fire Monkey: 1896, 1956

The Fire Monkey is intelligent, full of vitality, and has no trouble in commanding the respect of others. He is imaginative and has wide interests, although sometimes these can distract him from more useful and profitable work. He is very competitive and always likes to be involved in everything that is going on. He can be stubborn if he does not get his own way and he sometimes tries to indoctrinate those who are less strong-willed than himself. The Fire Monkey is a lively character, popular with the opposite sex and extremely loyal to his partner.

Earth Monkey: 1908, 1968

The Earth Monkey tends to be studious and well-read, and can become quite distinguished in his chosen line of work. He is less outgoing than some of the other types of Monkey and prefers quieter and more solid pursuits. He has high principles, a very caring nature, and can be most generous to those less fortunate than himself. He is usually successful in handling financial matters and can become very wealthy in old age. He has a calming influence on those around him and is respected and well liked by those he meets. He is, however, especially careful about whom he lets into his confidence.

Prospects for the Monkey in 1993

The Chinese New Year starts on 23 January 1993. Until then, the old year, the year of the Monkey, is still making its presence felt.

The year of the Monkey (4 February 1992 to 22 January 1993) is likely to have been a good year for the Monkey. He will have made a considerable amount of progress in many of his activities and will have greatly impressed those around him.

Even in the closing stages of the year much progress is possible, and the Monkey should continue to be on the look-out for new opportunities to pursue, particularly as far as his work is concerned. If he learns about an interesting new position or sees the chance of a new job or promotion he would do well to act. With a positive and concerted attitude, he will be delighted at what he is able to achieve at this time. Most Monkeys will find their reputation considerably enhanced in their own year and this will help their prospects in 1993.

The Monkey can also look forward to some most enjoyable times with his family and friends, and his social life in the closing stages of the year will be very busy. The Monkey is likely to have made some new and good friends over the year and these too will prove important to him in the future. Romance is also well aspected and for those who are unattached, there will be excellent opportunities towards the end of the Monkey year and early in the Rooster year to make new friends and build some long-lasting friendships.

Financial matters will generally go well, but the Monkey should still be careful not to commit any of his hard-earned money to risky ventures or to lend to others. If he does, he could experience problems in getting the loan repaid or will find a particularly speculative investment does not work out as well as he had hoped. Provided he is careful and prudent in money matters, he will do well.

The year of the Rooster starts on 23 January 1993 and is going to be a relatively pleasant year for the Monkey. Although not everything will go in his favour, he will still be able to end the year with some worthwhile gains to his credit. Throughout the year the Monkey will be helped by his ability to adapt to new situations and will see changes taking place in many aspects of his life.

In his work the Monkey is likely to be given new responsibilities and those around him will look favourably on his ideas and projects. He will find his colleagues most supportive over the year and this will be of great help to him. Throughout the year he should look for ways in which he can promote his skills and if he is seeking work or wishes to change his job, he should pursue the many opportunities that he will see over the year. Career matters are most favourably aspected in 1993.

The Monkey will also be reasonably fortunate when dealing with finance and most Monkeys will end the year in a better financial position than that in which they found themselves at the start. However, the Monkey can sometimes be guilty of trusting his luck too far and this is something he will need to watch in 1993. All Monkeys would do well to avoid committing themselves to speculative or risky ventures and should also be wary of 'too-good-to-be-true' offers. Despite the Monkey's perceptive nature, without care he could fall prey to some dubious schemes and offers, and this is something he should guard against.

Travel is well aspected in 1993, and most Monkeys will travel considerable distances. The Monkey is likely to find visits to countries and areas he has not visited before particularly interesting. However, in all the travelling he undertakes, it would be in his interest to plan his itinerary carefully in order to make the best use of his time away.

The Monkey can also look forward to leading a pleasant, although possibly expensive, social life over the year. There will be opportunities for new friendships and many

Monkeys will attend some most prestigious functions in 1993. However, with the many demands on his time that the Monkey will face in 1993, there is one area which he cannot afford to neglect, and that is his home life. There is a danger that the Monkey could become so preoccupied with his work and own concerns this year that he is not able to devote as much time to his family as he ought. This is something that he does need to watch, otherwise he could find domestic tensions arising. In order to avoid this, the Monkey would do well to take a keen interest in the activities of his family throughout the year, and make sure that he allows himself sufficient time to be with his loved ones. Providing he does this, he can look forward to some truly enjoyable times with his family and friends. He will also be grateful for the assistance and encouragement they are able to give him over the year, and if he does find himself under too many pressures at any time, he should not hesitate to seek the help of those around him.

The Monkey should also not let any disappointments or set-backs that he might experience over the year get the better of him. He has many good friends he can turn to for assistance, and with his resourceful and determined nature he will be able to overcome any problems that arise, and possibly even turn some of them to his advantage. The Monkey is renowned for his resourcefulness and in 1993 he will be able to put this talent to effective use.

Most Monkeys will enjoy outdoor pursuits over the year or derive much satisfaction from interests which allow them to use their imaginative and creative skills. However, all Monkeys should take extra care when lifting heavy objects and should follow all the precautions when using potentially dangerous pieces of equipment. A slip, strain or minor accident could cause the Monkey some discomfort which, with care, could have been avoided.

Generally, however, 1993 will be a relatively pleasant year for the Monkey. His career and financial prospects are certainly promising and he will enjoy many happy times.

Still, the Monkey would do well to try and spread his various commitments out over the year and he should also make sure that he devotes proper time and attention to his family and those around him.

As far as the different types of Monkey are concerned, this will be a rather mixed year for the **Metal Monkey**. Over the course of the year he could be faced with several important decisions to make and problems to overcome. Although these are unlikely to be serious, they could take the Metal Monkey some time to sort out satisfactorily. These decisions or problems are most likely to be related to changes in his accommodation or to making plans for his future. In arriving at any decisions and before taking any action, the Metal Monkey would do well to seek the advice of all those around him and to listen carefully to their views. To deal with any important or awkward matter single-handed could, as far as the Metal Monkey is concerned, only make matters worse and increase any pressure or burden that he is under. If he is prepared to be more open and avoid the temptation to be independent and, for some Metal Monkeys, stubborn, he will find things easier. However, despite any problems that do occur, the year will hold some very pleasant times for the Metal Monkey. He will thoroughly enjoy any short breaks or holidays that he takes and find these most beneficial for him. He will also find his various interests and hobbies most satisfying and he is likely to delight in the achievements of a close relation over the year. The second half of 1993 will be a much more fortunate time than the first half and by late summer the Metal Monkey will notice an upturn in his fortunes.

This will be a pleasant year for the **Water Monkey**. He will obtain considerable satisfaction from his various interests and hobbies over the year, and will find his work and business related interests will go well. Financial matters are also favourably aspected and many Water Monkeys can look forward to receiving a sum of money from the fruition of an investment or savings policy. However, despite any good fortune, the Water Monkey cannot afford to be complacent in financial matters and would do well to watch his general level of expenditure over the year. Any Water Monkey who finds he has spare time at his disposal will find a new interest or even a part-time job very satisfying and rewarding. Travel is also well aspected and the Water Monkey would do well to take any opportunity that he gets to visit relatives or friends living some distance away or to treat himself to a particularly special holiday. The Water Monkey will lead a generally content social and domestic life over the year, even though someone close to him could have a rather testing problem to overcome. Although he may not wish to seem interfering, the support and assistance that the Water Monkey is able to give will prove invaluable.

This will be a satisfying year for the **Wood Monkey**. He will be able to consolidate and build on any recent gains he has made, particularly in his work, and will impress those around him. There will also be opportunities to take on new responsibilities over the year or to move to a new position and, in both cases, the Wood Monkey will do well. The Wood Monkey will also be fortunate in financial matters, although he should try to avoid over-reaching himself. To stretch his resources too far could cause problems and he could find the repayment of any debts will take longer and prove more costly than he originally anticipated. Provided he is careful and prudent in his finances, however, he will do well. The Wood Monkey will lead a quiet but pleasant social life over the year, although he could experience a few domestic problems. These will not be serious but the Wood Monkey should try to tackle them as they arise and if he has any differences of opinion with those around him, he should sort the matter out as quickly and as amicably as he can. To let any problems or disagreements carry on throughout the year will only make matters worse, cause him additional worry and possibly take the edge off what could be a good year for him. In his relationships with others, the Wood Monkey should be open and frank. He should also involve those around him in his various projects as well as taking an interest in their activities. Travel is very well aspected for the Wood Monkey and he is likely to go on some very enjoyable and memorable journeys during the year.

Although not all the events of the year will be to the **Fire Monkey**'s liking, this will be a generally satisfying year for him and he can look forward to making progress in many of his activities. In his work he is likely to take on additional responsibilities or move to a new and more challenging position. However, to maximize these favourable trends, he does need to remain aware of all that is going on around him and listen closely to the views of his colleagues. He should also involve others as much as possible in his various plans and activities. If he maintains an independent attitude there is a danger that he could find himself isolated and lacking the support that he needs. The Fire Monkey's domestic life will be generally busy over the year, and his family and friends are likely to make many demands on his time. If the Fire Monkey finds these demands are getting too much for him, he should not hesitate to let others know and ask for assistance. To try to deal with things single-handed could leave him tired and irritable, and this would be in the interests of no-one. The Fire Monkey should also make sure that he allows himself time to devote to his own interests, particularly those which provide a break from his everyday routine. If he is able to take up a new hobby or interest – perhaps a suitable sporting activity – he will find this especially beneficial.

This will be an important and valuable year for the **Earth Monkey**. During the year he will have the opportunity to broaden his skills, and this will do much to enhance his prospects in the latter part of 1993 and in early 1994. He will also greatly impress his colleagues with his efficient and courteous manner, and this too will help his progress.

If he is able to go on any courses during the year that could give him an additional skill or qualification, he will find that this will prove a very useful asset in the future. The Earth Monkey will also be helped by giving some thought to his objectives over the next few years, and any plans and ideas that he draws up are likely to prove more significant than he may realize at the time. The Earth Monkey will be relatively fortunate in financial matters and any financial problems that he might have been experiencing will be considerably eased. However, the Earth Monkey still needs to exercise great care over his level of expenditure and cannot afford to be complacent over any large financial agreement or transaction he is about to enter into, especially one concerning property or a sizeable purchase. He should clarify the terms of any agreement he enters into and, if in doubt, seek reliable professional advice. The Earth Monkey will lead a busy social and domestic life over the year and will be much in demand with his family and friends. He can also look forward to attending some most enjoyable social functions over the year as well as being involved in a family celebration. In view of the generally busy nature of the year, the Earth Monkey would do well to ensure that he takes a proper holiday and regularly gives himself the chance to relax and unwind fully.

Famous Monkeys

Michael Aspel, Bobby Ball, J.M. Barrie, David Bellamy, Jacqueline Bisset, Bjorn Borg, Frank Bough, Faith Brown, Yul Brynner, Julius Caesar, Marti Caine, Princess Caroline of Monaco, Johnny Cash, Roy Castle, Sebastian Coe, John Constable, Alistair Cooke, Charles Dickens, Jonathan Dimbleby, Jason Donovan, Kenny Everett, Mia Farrow, Michael Fish, F. Scott Fitzgerald, Ian Fleming, Dick Francis, Paul Gauguin, Luke Goss, Matt Goss, Jerry Hall, Roy Hattersley, Stephen Hendry, Harry Houdini, Tony Jacklin,

P.D. James, Pope John Paul II, Lyndon B. Johnson, Edward Kennedy, Nigel Kennedy, Jonathan King, Cyndi Lauper, Nigel Lawson, Leo McKern, Walter Matthau, Princess Michael of Kent, Kylie Minogue, Martina Navratilova, Jack Nicklaus, Derek Nimmo, Peter O'Toole, Chris Patten, Mario Puzo, Tim Rice, Little Richard, Angela Rippon, Diana Ross, Omar Sharif, Wilbur Smith, Koo Stark, Rod Stewart, Michael Stich, Elizabeth Taylor, Graham Taylor, Dame Kiri Te Kanawa, Harry Truman, Leonardo da Vinci, Brian Walden, Norman Willis, Gary Wilmot, the Duchess of Windsor, Bobby Womack.

The Rooster

22 January 1909 to	9 February 1910	*Earth Rooster*
8 February 1921 to	27 January 1922	*Metal Rooster*
26 January 1933 to	13 February 1934	*Water Rooster*
13 February 1945 to	1 February 1946	*Wood Rooster*
31 January 1957 to	17 February 1958	*Fire Rooster*
17 February 1969 to	5 February 1970	*Earth Rooster*
5 February 1981 to	24 January 1982	*Metal Rooster*
23 January 1993 to	9 February 1994	*Water Rooster*

The Personality of the Rooster

Take calculated risks. That is quite different from being rash.

– George Patton: a Rooster.

The Rooster is born under the sign of candour. He has a flamboyant and colourful personality and is meticulous in all that he does. He is an excellent organizer and wherever possible likes to plan his various activities well in advance.

The Rooster is highly intelligent and usually very well read. He has a good sense of humour and is an effective and persuasive speaker. He loves discussion and enjoys taking part in any sort of debate. He has no hesitation in speaking his mind and is forthright in his views. He does, however, lack tact and can easily damage his reputation or cause offence by some thoughtless remark or action. The Rooster also has a very volatile nature, and he should always try to avoid acting on the spur of the moment.

The Rooster is usually very dignified in his manner and conducts himself with an air of confidence and authority. He is adept at handling financial matters and, as with most things, he organizes his financial affairs with considerable skill. He chooses his investments well and is capable of achieving great wealth. Most Roosters save or use their money wisely, but there are a few who are the reverse and are notorious spendthrifts. Fortunately, the Rooster has great earning capacity and is rarely without sufficient funds to tide himself over.

Another characteristic of the Rooster is that he invariably carries a notebook or scraps of paper around with him. He is constantly writing himself reminders or noting down important facts lest he forgets – the Rooster cannot abide inefficiency and conducts all his activities in an orderly, precise and methodical manner.

The Rooster is usually very ambitious, but can be unrealistic in some of the things that he hopes to achieve. He occasionally lets his imagination run away with him and, while he does not like any interference in the things that he does, it would be in his own interests if he were to listen to the views of others a little more often. He also does not like criticism, and if he feels anybody is doubting his judgement or prying too closely into his affairs, the Rooster is certain to let his feelings be known. He can also be rather self-centred and stubborn over relatively trivial matters, but to compensate for this he is reliable, honest and trustworthy, and this is very much appreciated by all who come into contact with him.

Roosters born between the hours of five and seven (both at dawn and sundown), tend to be the most extrovert of their sign, but all Roosters like to lead an active social life and enjoy attending parties and big functions. The Rooster usually has a wide circle of friends and is able to build up influential contacts with remarkable ease. He often belongs to several clubs and societies and involves himself in a

variety of different activities. He is particularly interested
in the environment, humanitarian affairs and anything
affecting the welfare of others. The Rooster has a very
caring nature and will do much to help those less fortunate
than himself.

He also gets much pleasure from gardening and, while
he may not spend as much time in the garden as he would
like, his garden is invariably well-kept and extremely
productive.

The Rooster is generally very distinguished in his
appearance and, if his job permits, he will wear an official
uniform with great pride and dignity. He is not averse to
publicity and takes great delight in being the centre of
attention. He often does well at PR work or any job which
brings him into contact with the media. He also makes a
very good teacher.

The lady Rooster leads a varied and interesting life. She
involves herself in many different activities and there are
some who wonder how she can achieve so much. The lady
Rooster often holds very strong views and, like her male
counterpart, has no hesitation in speaking her mind or
telling others how she thinks things should be done. She
is supremely efficient and well-organized and her home is
usually very neat and tidy. The lady Rooster has good taste
in clothes and usually wears smart but very practical
outfits.

The Rooster usually has a large family and as a parent
takes a particularly active interest in the education of his
children. He is very loyal to his partner and will find that
he is especially well-suited to those born under the signs
of the Snake, Horse, Ox and Dragon. Provided they do not
interfere too much in the Rooster's various activities the
Rat, Tiger, Goat and Pig can also establish a good
relationship with the Rooster, but two Roosters together are
likely to squabble and irritate each other. The rather
sensitive Rabbit will find the Rooster a bit too blunt for his
liking, and the Rooster will quickly become exasperated by

the ever-inquisitive and artful Monkey. The Rooster will also find it difficult to get on with the Dog.

If the Rooster can overcome his volatile nature and exercise more tact in some of the things that he says, he will go far in life. He is capable and talented and will invariably make a lasting – and usually favourable – impression almost everywhere he goes.

The Five Different Types of Rooster

In addition to the 12 signs of the Chinese zodiac, there are five elements and these have a strengthening or moderating influence on the sign. The effects of the five elements on the Rooster are described below, together with the years in which the elements were exercising their influence. Therefore all Roosters born in 1921 and 1981 are Metal Roosters, those born in 1933 and 1993 are Water Roosters, and so on.

Metal Rooster: 1921, 1981
The Metal Rooster is a hard and conscientious worker. He knows exactly what he wants in life and sets about everything he does in a positive and determined manner. He can at times appear abrasive and he would almost certainly do better if he were more willing to reach a compromise with others rather than hold so rigidly to his firmly held beliefs. He is very articulate and most astute when dealing with financial matters. He is loyal to his friends and often devotes much energy to working for the common good.

Water Rooster: 1933, 1993
This Rooster has a very persuasive manner and can easily gain the co-operation of others. He is intelligent, well-read, and gets much enjoyment from taking part in discussions and debates. He has a seemingly inexhaustible amount of

energy and is prepared to work long hours in order to secure what he wants. He can, however, waste much valuable time worrying over minor and inconsequential details. He is approachable, has a good sense of humour, and is highly regarded by others.

Wood Rooster: 1945
The Wood Rooster is honest, reliable and often sets himself high standards. He is ambitious, but also more prepared to work in a team than some of the other types of Rooster. He usually succeeds in life but does have a tendency to get caught up in bureaucratic matters or attempt too many things all at the same time. He has wide interests, likes to travel, and is very considerate and caring towards his family and friends.

Fire Rooster: 1897, 1957
This Rooster is extremely strong-willed. He has many leadership qualities, is an excellent organizer, and is most efficient in his work. Through sheer force of character he often secures his objectives, but he does have a tendency to be very forthright and not always consider the feelings of others. If the Fire Rooster can learn to be more tactful he can often succeed beyond his wildest dreams.

Earth Rooster: 1909, 1969
This Rooster has a deep and penetrating mind. He is extremely efficient, very perceptive, and is particularly astute in business and financial matters. He is also persistent, and once he has set himself an objective, he will rarely allow himself to be deflected from achieving his aim. The Earth Rooster works hard and is held in great esteem by his friends and colleagues. He usually gets much enjoyment from the arts and takes a keen interest in the activities of the various members of his family.

Prospects for the Rooster in 1993

The Chinese New Year starts on 23 January 1993. Until then, the old year, the year of the Monkey, is still making its presence felt.

The year of the Monkey (4 February 1992 to 22 January 1993) will have been a mixed year for the Rooster. Not all the events of the year will have gone as well as he would have liked and the Rooster could have found it difficult to make progress.

For what remains of the Monkey year, the Rooster would do well to exercise care, keep a close watch on all that is going on around him, and remain discreet and diplomatic. The Monkey year is just not a year when the Rooster can take risks, become complacent or afford to impair his relations with others. Caution and discretion are very much the by-words for the Rooster at this time. Providing he bears this in mind and continues to set about his activities in his usual conscientious manner, the work which he does will help to form the basis for the super progress he will make in his own year, the year of the Rooster.

Also, if the opportunity arises, the Rooster would do well to enrol on any courses that might be available to him and use any chance he gets to increase his experience and knowledge. Anything that the Rooster can do to add to his skills will repay him handsomely in the months and years ahead.

Over the Monkey year some Roosters may also have experienced problems in their domestic life, and where any problems or differences still remain, the Rooster would do well to use any opportunity that comes his way to sort the differences out in a sensible and conciliatory manner. Some of these problems may have arisen because the Rooster has been too preoccupied with his own activities and has not taken into account fully the interests of those around him. If the Rooster feels that this is the case, he should make every effort in the closing stages of the Monkey year to make amends and devote more time and attention to those close to him.

Although the Monkey year will not have been the best of years for the Rooster, he can nevertheless take comfort, for there will be a gradual improvement in his fortunes in the closing stages of the year and this improvement will gather pace in his own year.

The year of the Rooster starts on 23 January 1993 and will be a very good year for the Rooster. He can look forward to making considerable progress in many of his activities and this will help to make up for any disappointments that he might have suffered in recent years. Many Roosters will be imbued with great enthusiasm over the year and will be determined to realize their full potential. This change in attitude will certainly help the Rooster's progress and throughout 1993 he should be bold, positive and determined.

In the Rooster's work at this time there will be many opportunities to display his true skills and impress those around him. Those Roosters seeking work or aiming for promotion or a change of job should pursue any opportunities and openings they see. With a determined effort and the favourable trends that exist, their efforts will be rewarded. Many Roosters can expect some pleasing news concerning their work in the first half of the year.

However, despite the progress the Rooster can make in his career, he will still need to work hard in order to achieve the results he desires. He should also ensure that he has the support of others before embarking on any new scheme or project. Sometimes the Rooster can let his enthusiasm get the better of him and it would be a shame for him, in such an auspicious year, to waste valuable time on an enterprise only to find that he is lacking the support he needs. In 1993, planning, preparation and the support of others are vital to his success.

The Rooster will also be fortunate in financial matters over the year. Many Roosters can look forward to an increase in their income in 1993 and to a noticeable improvement in their financial situation. If the Rooster does have any spare funds at his disposal, he would do well to consider taking out a savings scheme or policy which would make provision for his long-term future. This could prove a valuable asset in years to come.

The Rooster will also have a greatly improved social life over the year. He can look forward to attending some enjoyable parties and functions and his circle of friends and acquaintances will widen considerably. Although matters of the heart may not run entirely smoothly for the single Rooster, any strain or difficulty that he might experience in a relationship can, with good common sense, be overcome and result in the relationship being put on a more solid foundation. For those Roosters seeking new friends, the spring and summer months are a particularly auspicious time for meeting others.

The Rooster will lead a content and settled domestic life in 1993. He will be grateful for the support and encouragement those around him will be able to give over the year. In return, actively involving himself in the interests of his family and friends will give both himself and his loved ones considerable pleasure and satisfaction.

The Rooster will enjoy any travelling he undertakes over the year and will also obtain much enjoyment from his various hobbies and interests. However, he does need to deal with forms and important correspondence with care and, as always, if he can curb his rather forthright and candid tongue, he will find life will run much more smoothly for him in general.

This will be very much a year of progress for the Rooster and providing he is prepared to work hard – which most Roosters do anyway – and he pursues his objectives with determination, his results over the year can be quite spectacular. However, to ensure his progress and success, the Rooster does need to make sure that he has the backing and support of others for any new plans or ideas that he has in mind.

As far as the different types of Rooster are concerned, 1993 will be a pleasing year for the **Metal Rooster**. He will lead an enjoyable social life and will be much in demand with his family and friends. For those Metal Roosters who may have been lonely or have recently moved, the prospects for making new friends are excellent, and socially this will be one of the happiest and most fulfilling years that the Metal Rooster has enjoyed for a long time. His hobbies and interests are also likely to be a great source of joy for him and the Metal Rooster will particularly enjoy outdoor pursuits over the year. He can also look forward to having some memorable times with his family in 1993 and the achievements of a close relation will be a great source of pride to him. He will be generally fortunate in financial matters and an interest or skill that he has could provide him with an additional source of income. If the Metal Rooster finds that he has any spare time at his disposal, he should seriously consider taking up another interest, preferably one that involves him mixing with others. He will find this most beneficial and it could also lead to some new and good friendships. Also, any Metal Rooster who may, in recent years, have had some sadness or major problems to contend with should look on 1993 as a year in which to make a new start. With the right attitude and the auspicious trends that exist, this can be an important year and one which will certainly mark an upturn in the Metal Rooster's fortunes.

This will be an important and memorable year for the **Water Rooster** and over the course of the year several significant changes could take place. Many Water Roosters will move or have some major alterations carried out on their property, and while this process could be disruptive, the end result will be very pleasing to the Water Rooster and well worth all the energy and possible frustration. However, before embarking on any move or committing himself to any new and major undertaking, the Water

Rooster would do well to keep a close watch on the costs and implications involved. Financial and business matters are, however, generally well aspected over the year and some work or project that the Water Rooster has been engaged on will bring him much praise and recognition. Travel is also well aspected in 1993 and is likely to prove both enjoyable and beneficial. This is a good year for the Water Rooster to visit distant relations or see friends that he has not met for a long time. The Water Rooster will obtain much pleasure from his various interests over the year and any Water Rooster who has literary or artistic skills should promote his work as much as he can. He will be delighted with how it is received. The Water Rooster can look forward to an active and pleasant social life over the year and his domestic life will be generally content and settled.

This will be a successful and enjoyable year for the **Wood Rooster**. He will make substantial progress in his work and should pursue any opportunities and openings he sees. Many Wood Roosters will be promoted during the year or obtain a new, challenging and more rewarding position. The opportunities for progress are excellent and it is up to the Wood Rooster to do all that he can to maximize these trends. The Wood Rooster will also be very fortunate in financial matters and should he find he has surplus funds at his disposal, it would be in his interest to consider making provision for his long-term future. He will also be lucky in some purchases that he makes over the year and if he has a hobby which involves collecting, he could make some excellent finds for any collection that he is building up. The Wood Rooster will lead a busy social life over the year and he is likely to impress those he meets and win ready support for his views and ideas. His family life too will be enjoyable and settled, although the Wood Rooster should make every effort to involve those around him in his activities and to devote time and attention to his loved ones. If not, relations could become strained and mar what will otherwise be an excellent year for him.

This will be a satisfying year for the **Fire Rooster**. If, in recent times, he has felt that his efforts have passed unnoticed or that he has not been making the progress he would have liked, this will change in 1993. Very early on in the year, the Fire Rooster will notice an improvement in his fortunes. There will be new opportunities for him to pursue, particularly in work matters, and many Fire Roosters will be given new and interesting responsibilities. Fire Roosters seeking work or wanting a change in their career should follow up any openings that they see even if, at the time, success may seem remote. With determination and a positive outlook, their efforts will bring pleasing results. However, despite the good fortune that the Fire Rooster will enjoy over the year, he will need to work hard and concentrate on specific objectives. Sometimes he can be over-zealous and take on too many commitments at any one time, and this is something he should guard against in 1993. The Fire Rooster will also do well in financial matters and he can look forward to a happy social and domestic life. The achievements of a younger relation will, in particular, give him much joy over the year. If the Fire Rooster does not get much exercise during the day, he will find a keep-fit course or some additional and suitable exercise will do much for his well-being. It will also help him to unwind from the pressures and tensions of everyday life.

This will be an enjoyable and fulfilling year for the **Earth Rooster**. His social and domestic life in particular will be most happy and many Earth Roosters will have cause for a major celebration over the year – they may get engaged or married or have a birth in their family. The Earth Rooster will also do well in academic and work matters, although throughout the year he should try to be realistic in his ambitions and not let his enthusiasm get the better of him. He can make substantial progress over the year, but it is very much a case of progressing steadily and surely rather than achieving all his goals straightaway. Also, if he is able to gain an additional skill or qualification over the year, this will be very much to his future advantage. There will, however, be some splendid opportunities for the Earth Rooster to advance in his career or to obtain a new job during the year and he would do well to go after any openings he sees. He will be generally fortunate in financial matters in 1993, although he should keep a close watch over his level of expenditure and try not too stretch his resources too far. The Earth Rooster can look forward to several strokes of luck over the year and could also be successful in a competition he enters.

Famous Roosters

Kate Adie, Dame Janet Baker, Severiano Ballesteros, Michael Bentine, Dirk Bogarde, Barbara Taylor Bradford, Julian Bream, Richard Briers, Michael Caine, Jasper Carrot, Enrico Caruso, Christopher Cazenove, Eric Clapton, Joan Collins, Edith Cresson, Leslie Crowther, Roger Daltry, Dickie Davies, Steve Davis, Les Dawson, Cathy Dennis, the Duke of Edinburgh, Gloria Estefan, Nick Faldo, Bryan Ferry, Errol Flynn, Stephen Fry, Steffi Graf, Richard Harris, Deborah Harry, Goldie Hawn, Katherine Hepburn, James Herbert, Michael Heseltine, Diane Keaton, Tom King, Bernhard Langer, D.H. Lawrence, Martyn Lewis, David Livingstone, Ken Livingstone, David McCallum, Steve Martin, W. Somerset Maugham, Van Morrison, Paul Nicholas, Barry Norman, Yoko Ono, Donny Osmond, Dolly Parton, Roman Polanski, Priscilla Presley, Nancy Reagan, Joan Rivers, Bobby Robson, Sir Harry Secombe, Carly Simon, Johann Strauss, Jacqueline Susann, Jayne Torvill, Sir Peter Ustinov, Richard Wagner.

The Dog

10 February 1910 to	29 January 1911	*Metal Dog*
28 January 1922 to	15 February 1923	*Water Dog*
14 February 1934 to	3 February 1935	*Wood Dog*
2 February 1946 to	21 January 1947	*Fire Dog*
18 February 1958 to	7 February 1959	*Earth Dog*
6 February 1970 to	26 January 1971	*Metal Dog*
25 January 1982 to	12 February 1983	*Water Dog*

The Personality of the Dog

All experience is an arch, to build upon.
– *Henry Brooks Adams: a Dog.*

The Dog is born under the signs of loyalty and anxiety. He usually holds very firm views and beliefs and is the champion of good causes. He hates any sort of injustice or unfair treatment and will do all in his power to help those less fortunate than himself. He has a strong sense of fair play and will be honourable and open in all his dealings.

The Dog is very direct and straightforward. He is never one to skirt round issues and speaks frankly and to the point. He can also be stubborn, but he is more than prepared to listen to the views of others and will try to be as fair as possible in coming to his decisions. He will readily give advice where it is needed and will be the first to offer assistance when things go wrong.

The Dog instils confidence wherever he goes and there

are many who admire him for his integrity and resolute manner. He is a very good judge of character and he can often form an accurate impression of someone very shortly after meeting them. He is also very intuitive and can frequently sense how things are going to work out long in advance.

Despite his friendly and amiable manner, the Dog is not a big socializer. He dislikes having to attend large social functions or parties and much prefers a quiet meal with friends or a chat by the fire. The Dog is an excellent conversationalist and is often a marvellous raconteur of amusing stories and anecdotes.

He is also quick-witted and his mind is always alert. He can keep calm in a crisis and although he does have a temper, his outbursts tend to be short-lived. The Dog is loyal and trustworthy, but if he ever feels badly let down or rejected by someone, he will rarely forgive or forget.

The Dog usually has very set interests. He prefers to specialize and become an expert in a chosen area rather than dabble in a variety of different activities. He usually does well in jobs where he feels that he is being of service to others and is often suited to careers in the social services, the medical and legal professions and teaching. The Dog does, however, need to feel motivated in his work. He has to have a sense of purpose in the things that he does and if ever this is lacking he can quite often drift through life without ever achieving very much. Once he has the motivation, however, very little can prevent him from securing his objective.

Another characteristic of the Dog is his tendency to worry and to view things rather pessimistically. Quite often these worries are totally unnecessary and are of his own making. Although it may be difficult, worrying is a habit which the Dog should try to overcome.

The Dog is not materialistic or particularly bothered about accumulating great wealth. As long as he has the necessary money to support his family and to spend on the occasional luxury, he is more than happy. However, when he does have any spare money the Dog tends to be rather a spendthrift and does not always put his money to its best use. He is also not a very good speculator and would be advised to get professional advice before entering into any major long-term investment.

The Dog will rarely be short of admirers, but he is not an easy person to live with. His moods are changeable and his standards high, but he will be loyal and protective to his partner and will do all in his power to provide her with a good and comfortable home. He can get on extremely well with those born under the signs of the Horse, Pig, Tiger and Monkey, and can also establish a sound and stable relationship with the Rat, Ox, Rabbit, Snake and another Dog, but will find the Dragon a bit too flamboyant for his liking. He will also find it difficult to understand the creative and imaginative Goat and is likely to get highly irritated by the candid Rooster.

The female Dog is renowned for her beauty. She has a warm and caring nature, although until she knows someone well she can be both secretive and very guarded. She is highly intelligent and despite her calm and tranquil appearance she can be extremely ambitious. She enjoys sport and other outdoor activities and has a happy knack of finding bargains in the most unlikely of places. The female Dog can also get rather impatient when things do not work out as she would like.

The Dog usually has a very good way with children and can be a loving and doting parent.

The Dog will rarely be happier than when he is helping someone or doing something that will benefit others. Providing he can cure himself of his tendency to worry, he will lead a very full and active life – and in that life he will make many friends and do a tremendous amount of good.

The Five Different Types of Dog

In addition to the 12 signs of the Chinese zodiac, there are five elements and these have a strengthening or moderating influence on the sign. The effects of the five elements on the Dog are described below, together with the years in which the elements were exercising their influence. Therefore all Dogs born in 1910 and 1970 are Metal Dogs, those born in 1922 and 1982 are Water Dogs, and so on.

Metal Dog: 1910, 1970
The Metal Dog is bold, confident and forthright, and sets about everything he does in a resolute and determined manner. He has a great belief in his abilities and has no hesitation about speaking his mind or devoting himself to some just cause. He can be rather serious at times and can get anxious and irritable when things are not going according to plan. He tends to have very specific interests and it would certainly help him to broaden his outlook and also become more involved in group activities. He is extremely loyal and faithful to his friends.

Water Dog: 1922, 1982
The Water Dog has a very direct and outgoing personality. He is an excellent communicator and has little trouble in persuading others to fall in with his plans. He does, however, have a somewhat carefree nature and is not as disciplined or as thorough as he should be in certain matters. Neither does he keep as much control over his finances as he should, but he can be most generous to his family and friends and will make sure that they want for nothing. The Water Dog is usually very good with children and has a wide circle of friends.

Wood Dog: 1934
This Dog is a hard and conscientious worker and will usually make a favourable impression wherever he goes. He

is less independent than some of the other types of Dog and prefers to work in a group rather than on his own. He is popular, has a good sense of humour, and takes a very keen interest in the activities of the various members of his family. He is often attracted to the finer things in life and can get much pleasure from collecting stamps, coins, pictures or antiques. He also prefers to live in the country to the town.

Fire Dog: 1946

This Dog has a lively, outgoing personality and is able to establish friendships with remarkable ease. He is an honest and conscientious worker and likes to take an active part in all that is going on around him. He also likes to explore new ideas and, providing he can get the necessary support and advice, he can often succeed where others have failed. He does, however, have a tendency to be stubborn. Providing he can overcome this, the Fire Dog can often achieve considerable fame and fortune.

Earth Dog: 1898, 1958

The Earth Dog is very talented and astute. He is methodical and efficient and is capable of going far in his chosen profession. He tends to be rather quiet and reserved but has a very persuasive manner and usually secures his objectives without too much opposition. He is generous and kind and is always ready to lend a helping hand when it is needed. He is also held in very high esteem by his friends and colleagues and he is usually most dignified in his appearance.

Prospects for the Dog in 1993

The Chinese New Year starts on 23 January 1993. Until then, the old year, the year of the Monkey, is still making its presence felt.

The year of the Monkey (4 February 1992 to 22 January 1993) is likely to have been a busy and demanding year for the Dog. Admittedly not all the events of the year will have gone as well as he would have liked, but his gains from the Monkey year could still be considerable. These gains could be in the form of a personal achievement, a broadening of his experience, or improvements in his work, finances or accommodation. Also, the events of the year will have helped strengthen the Dog's resolve and sense of purpose, and these qualities are all very important to the Dog personality.

The latter part of the Monkey year will also be an active time for the Dog and there could be quite a few matters in his work and round the home which require his attention. However, with a determined and organized approach, he will be well pleased with what he is able to accomplish at this time. When the Dog sets his mind to a task, very little will prevent him from achieving his objective, and this is how it will be in the closing stages of the Monkey year.

The Dog will also lead an active social life around the Christmas and the New Year holidays. He should use any opportunity he can get to rest and unwind from the exertions of the Monkey year and also to spend time with his family. For some Dogs, the demands over the Monkey year will have been so great that they may not always have paid as much attention to family matters as perhaps they should have done, and the holiday period would be an ideal time to rectify this.

The year of the Rooster starts on 23 January 1993 and is going to be a varied year for the Dog. While he can look forward to success in some aspects of his life, other areas do need careful attention. However, the problems and difficulties that arise need not spoil the year, and the progress and achievements that the Dog will make will serve him well in the future, particularly in 1994, his own year.

During 1993 the Dog can expect to make a moderate

amount of progress in his work. However, throughout the year, he should take a careful note of all that is going on around him and keep in touch with the views of his colleagues. If he finds himself in any contentious discussion, he would do well to remain diplomatic and tactful – to inflame the feelings of his work-fellows could be to his detriment. He would also do well to make sure that he has the support and backing of others before embarking on any major new enterprise. To retain an independent and 'go-it-alone' attitude could limit the success he would otherwise obtain. Provided he bears this in mind and continues to work to the best of his abilities, he will make steady progress over the year. It would also be useful for the Dog, either in work or seeking work, to try to add to his skills over the year. This could either be by enrolling on a course or by obtaining some sort of practical experience. He will find that this will do much to enhance his future prospects.

The Dog does, however, need to be careful with financial matters over the year and should avoid getting involved in any highly speculative activities. This is just not the right year to take financial risks and he should, as far as possible, avoid lending money to others. If he does, the Dog could easily end up the poorer. However, providing he retains a close watch over his level of spending and avoids risky undertakings, all will be well.

Matters of a bureaucratic nature also need care, particularly any important correspondence the Dog receives or forms he has to complete. There is a chance that the Dog could find himself in an awkward situation over the year, and naturally anything that he can do to avert a possible misinterpretation of a form he has completed or a letter he has written would be very much to his advantage.

The Dog will generally lead a pleasant domestic and social life over the year. He will find his family and friends ready to support him in his various undertakings but, in return, he should try to be more open and be prepared to discuss his feelings and plans. Sometimes the Dog has a tendency to keep his thoughts and ideas to himself and this is something he would do well to avoid in 1993. If he is more open he will find that others are better able to assist him and it will also help strengthen the rapport that he enjoys with those around him.

The Dog should also ensure that he involves himself in the interests of the various members of his family and does not get too preoccupied with his own concerns. If he does, he could find misunderstandings and tensions developing, which, with a bit of forethought, could have been avoided.

The single Dog will lead a pleasant social life and for those seeking romance and friendship, the spring and summer months will provide several excellent opportunities for meeting others.

Any travelling that the Dog undertakes in 1993 is likely to go well, although many Dogs are more likely to stay nearer to home than go on lengthy journeys. All Dogs should, however, make sure that they go away for one holiday over the year and give themselves a proper break from their usual everyday routine.

The Dog should also try to make sure that he does put some time aside for recreational pursuits and does not drive himself relentlessly, as some Dogs tend to do. If the Dog has a hobby that enables him to relax and unwind he should make sure that he allows himself some time to devote to it. Or, if he does not have such an interest, he would do well to consider taking one up. He will find that it will prove most beneficial for him as well as giving him much satisfaction and pleasure.

Although the year of the Rooster will not be the best of years for the Dog, it will not be a bad year either. The problems that he has to face are more nigglesome and annoying than serious. Providing he handles his relations with others with care and continues to work to the best of his abilities, the Dog's work and accomplishments over the year will put him in a good place to benefit from the greatly

improved trends that will occur in the latter part of the
Rooster year and which will remain with him in 1994.

As far as the different types of Dog are concerned, the
year of the Rooster will be an important and challenging
year for the **Metal Dog**. Not all the events of the year are
likely to work out in his favour, and he could be involved
in problems of a bureaucratic nature or find that his
relations with others need careful handling. However, the
Metal Dog is sufficiently astute to deal with the problems
that do emerge sensibly and could even turn a set-back that
he experiences to his long-term advantage. In this respect,
the experiences of the year will prove an important lesson
for the Metal Dog and will help strengthen and improve his
character. Another important aspect of the year is that it
will give the Metal Dog a good opportunity to examine his
present position and give some thought to his future,
especially his career. He would do well to talk to those with
experience and seek the guidance of others with regards to
his future plans. Indeed, the ideas and advice that the Metal
Dog obtains over the year will prove most helpful in the
not too distant future. The Metal Dog can, however, look
forward to some memorable times with his family and
friends over the year and his social life will be most
pleasant. He will also derive particular pleasure from
outdoor activities, or from interests which allow him to
meet and mix with others. Many Metal Dogs will change
their accommodation over the year and providing they are
careful over all the costs and financial implications of any
agreement they enter into, their move will work out well
for them.

This will be a pleasant if not outstanding year for the
Water Dog. His domestic life is likely to give him much
pleasure and he can look forward to some enjoyable times
with his family and friends. However, over the course of the
year, he may be called upon to assist someone close to him
who has an awkward problem to overcome. Any help that
the Water Dog can offer will prove of great assistance and

be much appreciated. The Water Dog will also derive considerable satisfaction from his hobbies and interests in 1993 and for those who enjoy gardening or out-of-door activities, the year will hold many satisfying moments. Also, any Water Dog who has artistic or creative talents should promote his work as much as he can, as it is likely to be favourably received. The Water Dog should, however, be cautious when dealing with financial matters and be particularly wary about lending money to others. Also, on a cautionary note, he should take every precaution necessary before using potentially dangerous pieces of equipment and be careful when moving heavy objects. The Water Dog will, however, greatly enjoy several short breaks and holidays that he takes during the year, particularly one arranged at fairly short notice.

This will be a pleasant but busy year for the **Wood Dog**. There will be many demands on his time and matters which require his attention. In view of this, the Wood Dog should avoid taking on too many commitments at any one time and would do well to spread his activities out throughout the year. If, however, he does find he has too much to tackle at any one time, he should not hesitate to ask for assistance from those around him. The Wood Dog will also be helped by setting about his various undertakings in a methodical manner and giving himself some priorities for the year. As far as his work is concerned, the Wood Dog could be successful in gaining a new job in the early part of 1993 or could be given new and more interesting responsibilities. He will have some most pleasant times with his family and will derive much pleasure from his various interests. Although this will be a busy year for him, the Wood Dog will generally be pleased with his achievements in 1993 and he can also look forward to several strokes of luck, especially in a competition he enters or in the fruition of a successful investment.

This will be a varied year for the **Fire Dog**. Over the year he could have some problems to overcome – particularly of a bureaucratic nature or involving a difference of opinion with someone – and, while not serious, these could prevent the Fire Dog from making as much progress as he would like. He could also find that some of his ideas and plans do not work out in the manner he would have liked, and this too could prove disappointing. However, 1993 will be an important year for the Fire Dog. By overcoming any problems that he has to face and by demonstrating his skills of diplomacy and strength of character, he will greatly impress others, and will emerge from the year in a strong position from which to progress. Yet throughout the year he should make sure that he acts with the support and backing of others and does not distance himself too much from all that is going on around him. The Fire Dog will also need to be careful in financial matters over the year. He will, however, lead a generally pleasant and active social life in 1993 and will attend some enjoyable functions. His family life too will be content and settled, and by involving those close to him in his activities, the Fire Dog will be gratified by the support and encouragement he is given. Any holidays and short breaks that he takes will prove especially beneficial for him and if his usual daytime activities do not allow him to get much exercise, he will find a suitable keep-fit course, or some activity such as walking or swimming will do much for his well-being. The Fire Dog will notice an upturn in his fortunes in the latter part of the year and the considerable progress that he will make next year will amply compensate for any difficulties that might have occurred in 1993.

This will be a demanding year for the **Earth Dog** and over the course of the year he is likely to face several decisions which will have an important bearing on his future. These could concern a change in his career or accommodation. However, before reaching any firm decision or taking any decisive action, the Earth Dog should seek the views of those around him and avoid taking any hasty action. The Earth Dog is by nature cautious and it is through his cautious and measured approach that he obtains the best results. Once he is sure in his own mind that a change, whether it concerns his work, accommodation or some other matter, is really what he wants, then he can proceed with confidence. Should he meet with any set-backs or reversals over the year, he should treat these as obstacles to overcome and triumph over, and indeed the experience that he gains over the year will hold him in good stead for the success that awaits him in 1994. The Earth Dog does, however, need to be careful in financial matters and would do well to keep a close watch over his general level of expenditure. Family matters will also keep him busy and while at some time during 1993 he may have some misgivings about the activities of a close relation, generally those around him will be a great source of pride, joy and support to him over the year.

Famous Dogs

Kingsley Amis, Jane Asher, Kenneth Baker, Brigitte Bardot, Christiaan Barnard, Candice Bergman, Lionel Blair, Simon le Bon, Betty Boo, David Bowie, Peter Brooke, Kate Bush, Max Bygraves, King Carl Gustaf XVI of Sweden, Belinda Carlisle, Cher, Sir Winston Churchill, Leonard Cohen, Robin Cook, Henry Cooper, Edwina Currie, Jamie Lee Curtis, Timothy Dalton, Charles Dance, Christopher Dean, Claude Debussy, John Dunn, Sally Field, Zsa Zsa Gabor, Judy Garland, Bamber Gascoigne, George Gershwin, Lenny Henry, Patricia Hodge, Frankie Howerd, Victor Hugo, Barry Humphries, Michael Jackson, Henry Kelly, Felicity Kendal, Nik Kershaw, Sue Lawley, Maureen Lipman, Sophia Loren, Joanna Lumley, Shirley MacLaine, Madonna, Norman Mailer, Barry Manilow, Rik Mayall, Simon Mayo, Golda Meir, Freddie Mercury, Liza Minnelli, David Niven, Gary Numan, Michelle Pfeiffer, Sydney Pollack, Elvis Presley, Anneka Rice, Malcolm Rifkind, Paul Robeson, Linda Ronstadt,

Gabriela Sabatini, Carl Sagan, Jennifer Saunders, Norman Schwarzkopf, Sylvester Stallone, Robert Louis Stevenson, David Suchet, Donald Sutherland, Mother Teresa, Voltaire, Timothy West, Mary Whitehouse, Prince William, Ian Woosnam.

The Pig

30 January 1911 to	17 February 1912	*Metal Pig*
16 February 1923 to	4 February 1924	*Water Pig*
4 February 1935 to	23 January 1936	*Wood Pig*
22 January 1947 to	9 February 1948	*Fire Pig*
8 February 1959 to	27 January 1960	*Earth Pig*
27 January 1971 to	14 February 1972	*Metal Pig*
13 February 1983 to	1 February 1984	*Water Pig*

The Personality of the Pig

Life is a series of experiences, each one of which makes us bigger, even though sometimes it is hard to realize this.

– Henry Ford: a Pig.

The Pig is born under the sign of honesty. He has a kind and understanding nature and is well-known for his abilities as a peace-maker. He hates any sort of discord or unpleasantness and will do all in his power to sort out differences of opinion or bring opposing factions together.

He is an excellent conversationalist and speaks truthfully and to the point. He dislikes any form of falsehood or hypocrisy and is a firm believer in justice and the maintenance of law and order. In spite of these beliefs, however, the Pig is reasonably tolerant and often prepared to forgive others for their wrongs. The Pig rarely harbours grudges and is never vindictive.

The Pig is usually very popular. He enjoys other people's company and likes to be involved in joint or group activities. He will be a loyal member of any club or society and can be relied upon to lend a helping hand at functions. He is also an excellent fund-raiser for charities and is often a great supporter of humanitarian causes.

The Pig is a hard and conscientious worker and is particularly respected for his reliability and integrity. In his early years he will try his hand at several different jobs, but he is usually happiest where he feels that he is being of service to others. He will unselfishly give up his time for the common good and is highly-valued by his colleagues and employers.

The Pig has a good sense of humour and invariably has a smile, joke or some whimsical remark at the ready. He loves to entertain and to please others, and there are many who have been attracted to careers in show business or who enjoy following the careers of famous stars and personalities.

There are, unfortunately, some who take advantage of the Pig's good nature and impose on his generosity. The Pig has great difficulty in saying 'no' and, although he may dislike being firm, it would be in his own interests to say occasionally, 'Enough is enough.' The Pig can also be rather naïve and gullible; if at any stage in his life he feels that he has been badly let down, he will make sure that it will never happen again and will try to become self-reliant. There are many Pigs who have become entrepreneurs or forged a successful career on their own after some early disappointment in life. And although the Pig tends to spend his money quite freely, he is usually very astute in financial matters and there are many Pigs who have become wealthy.

Another characteristic of the Pig is his ability to recover from set-backs reasonably quickly. His faith and his strength of character keep him going. If he thinks that there is a job he can do – or has something that he wants to achieve – he will pursue it with a dogged determination.

He can also be stubborn and, no matter how many may plead with him, once he has made his mind up he will rarely change his views.

Although the Pig may work hard, he also knows how to enjoy himself. He is a great pleasure-seeker and will quite happily spend his hard-earned money on a lavish holiday or an expensive meal – for the Pig is a connoisseur of good food and wine – or take part in a variety of recreational activities. He also enjoys small social gatherings and, if he is in company which he likes, the Pig can very easily become the life and soul of the party. He does, however, tend to become rather withdrawn at larger functions or when among strangers.

The Pig is also a creature of comfort and his home will usually be fitted with all the latest in luxury appliances. Where possible, he will prefer to live in the country to the town and will opt to have a big garden, for the Pig is usually a keen and successful gardener.

The Pig is very popular with the opposite sex and will often have numerous romances before he settles down. Once settled, however, he will be loyal and protective to his partner and he will find that he is especially well-suited to those born under the signs of the Goat, Rabbit, Dog and Tiger, and also to another Pig. Due to his affable and easy-going nature he can also establish a satisfactory relationship with all the remaining signs of the Chinese zodiac, with the exception of the Snake. The Snake tends to be wily, secretive and very guarded, and this can be intensely irritating to the honest and open-hearted Pig.

The lady Pig will devote all her energies to the needs of her children and her partner. She tries to ensure that they want for nothing and their pleasure is very much her pleasure. Her home will either be very clean and orderly or hopelessly untidy. Strangely, there seems to be no in-between with the Pig – they either love housework or detest it! The lady Pig does, however, have considerable talents as an organizer and this, combined with her friendly and open manner, enables her to secure many of her objectives. She can also be a caring and conscientious parent and has very good taste in clothes.

The Pig is usually lucky in life and will rarely want for anything. Provided he does not let others take advantage of his good nature and is not afraid of asserting himself, the Pig will go through life making friends, helping others and winning the admiration of many.

The Five Different Types of Pig

In addition to the 12 signs of the Chinese zodiac, there are five elements and these have a strengthening or moderating influence on the sign. The effects of the five elements on the Pig are described below, together with the years in which the elements were exercising their influence. Therefore all Pigs born in 1911 and 1971 are Metal Pigs, those born in 1923 and 1983 are Water Pigs, and so on.

Metal Pig: 1911, 1971
The Metal Pig is more ambitious and determined than some of the other types of Pig. He is strong, energetic and likes to be involved in a wide variety of different activities. He is very open and forthright in his views, although he can be a little too trusting at times and has a tendency to accept things at face value. He has a good sense of humour and loves to attend parties and other social gatherings. He has a warm, outgoing nature and usually has a large circle of friends.

Water Pig: 1923, 1983
The Water Pig has a heart of gold. He is generous and loyal and tries to remain on good terms with everyone. He will do his utmost to help others, but sadly there are some who will take advantage of his kind nature and he should, in his own interests, be a little more discriminating and be

prepared to stand firm against anything that he does not like. Although he prefers the quieter things in life, he has a wide range of interests. He particularly enjoys outdoor pursuits and attending parties and social occasions. He is a hard and conscientious worker and invariably does well in his chosen profession. He is also gifted in the art of communication.

Wood Pig: 1935
This Pig has a friendly, persuasive manner and is easily able to gain the confidence of others. He likes to be involved in all that is going on around him and can sometimes take on more responsibility than he can properly handle. He is loyal to his family and friends and he also derives much pleasure from helping those less fortunate than himself. The Wood Pig is usually an optimist and leads a very full, enjoyable and satisfying life. He also has a good sense of humour.

Fire Pig: 1947
The Fire Pig is both energetic and adventurous and he sets about everything he does in a confident and resolute manner. He is very forthright in his views and does not mind taking risks in order to achieve his objectives. He can, however, get carried away by the excitement of the moment and ought to exercise more caution with some of the enterprises in which he gets involved. The Fire Pig is usually lucky in money matters and is well-known for his generosity. He is also very caring towards the members of his family.

Earth Pig: 1899, 1959
This Pig has a kindly nature. He is sensible and realistic and will go to great lengths in order to please his employers and to secure his aims and ambitions. He is an excellent organizer and is particularly astute in business and financial matters. He has a good sense of humour and a wide circle of friends. He also likes to lead an active social life, although

he does sometimes have a tendency to eat and drink more than is good for him.

Prospects for the Pig in 1993

The Chinese New Year starts on 23 January 1993. Until then, the old year, the year of the Monkey, is still making its presence felt.

The year of the Monkey (4 February 1992 to 22 January 1993) is likely to have been a reasonable year for the Pig. Some aspects of his life will have gone very well, but in other areas he could have met with problems and these could have prevented him from making as much progress as he would have liked.

Socially and romantically, the year of the Monkey is a highly favourable year for the Pig, and there are certainly some good and happy times aspected for the closing stages of the year. The Pig will be invited to several most enjoyable social functions over the holiday period and for those seeking new friends or romance, December 1992 and the first few months of 1993 is a very auspicious time for meeting others, sometimes in most unusual circumstances.

For what remains of the Monkey year the Pig should, however, exercise prudence in financial matters and continue to set about his work and daily activities to the best of his abilities. Although work matters may not have gone as well as he may have wished, there will be a distinct improvement in the next 12 months. In view of this, the Pig cannot afford to slacken his efforts now. For the Pig with creative leanings this is, however, a good time to promote his talents and to bring his work to the attention of others. The Pig will also have several pleasant surprises in the closing stages of the Monkey year and this could even include winning a prize or receiving a very special and unexpected gift from someone.

The year of the Rooster starts on 23 January 1993 and is

going to be a pleasing year for the Pig. He will find that his past efforts and work will be recognized and that he will be able to obtain the results that may have been eluding him in recent years.

In his work the Pig can look forward to making considerable progress. This could be in the form of a new job or promotion and an increase in responsibilities. Throughout the year the Pig should be alert for opportunities to pursue and openings to follow. By being bold and assertive, he can make great progress, particularly in the early part of the year. If, however, the Pig should meet with any problems in work issues, he would do well to be patient. The aspects are highly favourable for him in career matters and he will find his patience and perseverance rewarded as the year progresses.

This will, however, be a generally busy year for the Pig and as far as possible he should spread his activities out over the course of the year. He should also be wary of getting involved in too many commitments at any one time. If he finds he has a particularly heavy work load, he should not hesitate to ask for assistance from others. He will find those around him willing to co-operate and support him and it is up to the Pig to ask for assistance if he finds he is under too much pressure. Despite his generally very obliging and co-operative nature, it would be in his interests to set a sensible limit on the number of his undertakings, especially if he feels he cannot give the proper time and attention to whatever is being asked of him.

The Pig will be fortunate in financial matters in 1993 and almost all Pigs will notice an improvement in their financial position over the year. However, despite any financial good fortune he may enjoy, the Pig cannot be lulled into a false sense of complacency. He still needs to handle financial matters with care and even though many Pigs have a rather indulgent nature, the Pig should avoid squandering any spare money away needlessly. He could find any money that he has accumulated particularly useful in the latter part

of the year, especially in financing home improvements,
travel or an expensive item he wishes to purchase.

The Pig will lead a most enjoyable domestic and social
life in 1993. He can look forward to having some happy
times with his family and his domestic life will be generally
content and settled. Many Pigs will find their circle of
friends and acquaintances will widen appreciably over the
year. It is also a most auspicious year for romance.

Another area which is also well aspected is recreational
pursuits. This is a good year for the Pig to 'do his own
thing'. If he has thought about going on a long journey or
spending time visiting another country, this would be a
good year to do so. Alternatively, if there is some interest
or hobby that the Pig has thought of taking up, again he
would do well to follow this through. Almost all Pigs will
derive considerable satisfaction and benefit from devoting
time to their own pursuits and interests over the year. In
addition to the pleasure this will give the Pig, it will help
him to relax and unwind from everyday pressures.

Generally, 1993 will be a busy but pleasing year for the
Pig. There will be new opportunities to pursue and the Pig
will be able to make considerable progress in most of his
activities. In addition to this, his family and social life will
also be enjoyable. Providing he does not over-commit
himself in financial matters or is extravagant in his
spending, this will be one of the most successful and
rewarding years that the Pig has enjoyed for a long time.

As far as the different types of Pig are concerned, 1993
will be a fulfilling year for the **Metal Pig**. He can look
forward to making considerable progress in his work and
many Metal Pigs will be successful in gaining a new job or
being promoted. The Metal Pig will greatly impress those
around him and his accomplishments and the experience
that he gains in 1993 will prove of great importance in years
to come. The Metal Pig will be generally fortunate in
financial matters, although he would do well to keep a
watchful eye over his level of spending. His personal life

will, however, be most enjoyable. He can look forward to having some memorable times with his family as well as leading a busy social life. Many Metal Pigs who are unattached are likely to meet their future partner over the year and the aspects for romance, engagement and marriage are most favourable. Generally the Metal Pig will be well pleased with his accomplishments in 1993. However, in all that he does, he should adopt a positive frame of mind, and even if he does occasionally meet with a set-back or disappointment, he should allow this to strengthen his resolve. For the bold, determined and forward-thinking Metal Pig, this will be a year of great progress.

This will be an important year for the **Water Pig** and during the course of it he could take several decisions which will have a significant bearing on his future. These could concern almost any aspect of his life, but could particularly relate to accommodation or, for those Water Pigs in education, a possible change of school. In either case, the Water Pig should not rush into any irrevocable decision but should carefully consider all the options available to him and also seek the advice of those around him. By taking his time and satisfying himself in his own mind that the decision is the right one, he can move forward with confidence and will be pleased with how things work out. The Water Pig does, however, need to be careful in financial matters and should be wary of committing himself to any undertaking that would stretch his resources too far. Again, if he has any doubts over any financial matter with which he is involved, he would do well to seek reliable professional advice. The Water Pig can look forward to some memorable times with his family and friends in 1993 and his social life will be generally most enjoyable. Any travelling that he undertakes will go well and a holiday taken in the autumn will prove most beneficial for him and could also lead to some new friendships.

This will be a positive and fulfilling year for the **Wood Pig**. He will be much in demand with his family and friends and will lead a busy and enjoyable social life. A younger relation in particular will be a great source of pride to him. However, if any of his relations or close friends experience problems over the year or seek the Wood Pig's advice, he would do well to lend what assistance he can but at the same time speak truthfully and honestly rather than concealing his true opinions. His assistance and advice will be greatly appreciated and will do much to help. He will also derive much pleasure from his interests over the year and any Wood Pig who finds he has some spare time at his disposal should seriously consider either taking up a new interest or learning a new skill. He will find this will prove both satisfying and also potentially most rewarding for him. The Wood Pig will enjoy considerable success in work matters and he could be rewarded for past achievements by promotion, an unexpected bonus or by an increase in salary. The Wood Pig does, however, need to exercise care when dealing with financial matters and should avoid committing himself to any risky or highly speculative venture. Any travelling the Wood Pig undertakes over the year will go well and his main holiday will prove most enjoyable.

This will be a good although rather demanding year for the **Fire Pig**. He can look forward to making substantial progress in his work and any Fire Pig seeking a new job would do well to pursue any new openings he sees. Also, if there is any opportunity for the Fire Pig to broaden his skills, either by going on a course or by setting aside time for private study, his efforts will be greatly rewarded and will do much to enhance his prospects. The Fire Pig will also lead quite an active social life over the year and he will meet and impress several people who will be able to help his progress over the next few years. Financial matters are well aspected, and if the Fire Pig should have any spare funds at his disposal, he would do well to consider taking out a policy which would make provision for his longer-term future. Family matters will also go well, although to preserve domestic harmony the Fire Pig should be prepared to discuss his feelings and views openly and make every effort to involve himself in the activities of those around him. He would also do well to make sure that he sets some time aside for his own interests, particularly those which allow him to unwind from everyday pressures. Also, if he does not get much exercise during the day, he will find that walking, swimming or some other suitable excrcise will do much to improve his well-being. One word of caution though – throughout the year, the Fire Pig does need to exercise care when handling heavy or dangerous pieces of equipment. A strain or accident could result in needless suffering.

This will be an enjoyable and satisfying year for the **Earth Pig**. His family and friends will be a great source of pleasure for him over the year and he will find that those around him will give him much useful support and encouragement. In addition to his domestic life being content and settled, he will lead a most pleasing social life with the prospects of new friends and some memorable functions to attend. Work matters will also go well, and while the Earth Pig may sometimes feel that his talents and efforts are going unnoticed, this is not the case. He will greatly impress others in 1993 and many Earth Pigs can look forward to promotion or a new job during the year. The Earth Pig does, however, need to watch his general level of spending in 1993 and he will find a few prudent alterations to his current level of outgoings will lead to a substantial improvement in his financial situation. He should, however, avoid taking risks in money matters and make sure that he understands all the implications of any financial undertakings that he commits himself to over the year. The Earth Pig will particularly enjoy outdoor pursuits in 1993 and for those who enjoy sport, gardening or travelling, the year will hold many happy and satisfying moments.

Famous Pigs

Russ Abbot, Woody Allen, Julie Andrews, Fred Astaire, Sir Richard Attenborough, Simon Bates, Jeremy Beadle, Gerhard Berger, Humphrey Bogart, Maria Callas, Dr George Carey, Brian Clough, Sir Noël Coward, Oliver Cromwell, the Dalai Lama, Sir Robin Day, Lord Denning, Richard Dreyfuss, Sheena Easton, Ralph Waldo Emerson, David Essex, Farrah Fawcett, Henry Ford, Debbie Greenwood, Emmylou Harris, Chesney Hawkes, William Randolph Hearst, Ernest Hemingway, Henry VIII, Alfred Hitchcock, King Hussein of Jordan, Elton John, C.G. Jung, Stephen King, Henry Kissinger, Jerry Lee Lewis, John McEnroe, Marcel Marceau, Ngaio Marsh, Johnny Mathis, Robert Maxwell, Montgomery of Alamein, Dudley Moore, Patrick Moore, John Mortimer, Wolfgang Amadeus Mozart, Michael Parkinson, Luciano Pavarotti, Lester Piggott, Maurice Ravel, Dan Quayle, Ronald Reagan, John D. Rockefeller, Ginger Rogers, Nick Ross, Sade, Salman Rushdie, Baroness Sue Ryder of Warsaw, Arantxa Sanchez, Telly Savalas, Arnold Schwarzenegger, Albert Schweitzer, Donald Sinden, Steven Spielberg, Tracey Ullman, the Duchess of York.

Appendix

The relationship between the 12 animal signs – both on a personal level and business level – is an important aspect of Chinese horoscopes and in this Appendix the compatibility between the signs is shown in the two tables that follow. Also included are the names of the signs ruling the hours of the day and from this it is possible to find your ascendant and discover yet another aspect of your personality.

Personal Relationships

Key
1 Excellent. Great rapport.
2 A successful relationship. Many interests in common.
3 Mutual respect and understanding. A good relationship.
4 Fair. Needs care and some willingness to compromise in order for the relationship to work.
5 Awkward. Possible difficulties in communication with few interests in common.
6 A clash of personalities. Very difficult.

	Rat	Ox	Tiger	Rabbit	Dragon	Snake	Horse	Goat	Monkey	Rooster	Dog	Pig
Rat	1											
Ox	1	3										
Tiger	4	6	5									
Rabbit	5	2	3	3								
Dragon	1	5	5	3	2							
Snake	3	1	6	2	1	5						
Horse	6	5	1	4	3	4	2					
Goat	5	5	3	1	4	3	2	2				
Monkey	1	3	6	3	1	3	5	3	1			
Rooster	4	1	4	6	2	1	2	4	5	5		
Dog	3	4	1	3	6	3	2	5	3	5	2	
Pig	2	3	2	2	3	6	3	2	2	3	1	2

Business Relationships

Key
1 Excellent. Marvellous understanding and rapport.
2 Very good. Complement each other well.
3 A good working relationship and understanding can be developed.
4 Fair, but compromise and a common objective is often needed to make this relationship work.
5 Awkward. Unlikely to work, either through lack of trust, understanding or the competitiveness of the signs.
6 Mistrust. Difficult. To be avoided.

	Rat	Ox	Tiger	Rabbit	Dragon	Snake	Horse	Goat	Monkey	Rooster	Dog	Pig
Rat	2											
Ox	1	3										
Tiger	3	6	5									
Rabbit	4	3	4	3								
Dragon	1	4	3	4	3							
Snake	3	2	6	4	1	5						
Horse	6	4	1	4	3	4	3					
Goat	4	5	3	1	4	3	3	2				
Monkey	2	3	4	5	1	5	4	4	3			
Rooster	5	1	5	5	2	1	2	5	4	6		
Dog	4	5	2	3	6	3	2	5	3	5	3	
Pig	3	3	2	2	4	5	4	2	3	4	3	3

Your Ascendant

The ascendant has a very strong influence on your personality and together with the information already given about your sign and the effects of the element on your sign, it will help you gain even greater insight into your true personality according to Chinese horoscopes.

The hours of the day are named after the 12 animal signs and the sign governing the time you were born is your ascendant. To find your ascendant, look up the time of your birth on the table below, bearing in mind any local time differences in the place you were born.

11 p.m. to	1 a.m.	The hours of the Rat
1 a.m. to	3 a.m.	The hours of the Ox
3 a.m. to	5 a.m.	The hours of the Tiger
5 a.m. to	7 a.m.	The hours of the Rabbit
7 a.m. to	9 a.m.	The hours of the Dragon
9 a.m. to	11 a.m.	The hours of the Snake
11 a.m. to	1 p.m.	The hours of the Horse
1 p.m. to	3 p.m.	The hours of the Goat
3 p.m. to	5 p.m.	The hours of the Monkey
5 p.m. to	7 p.m.	The hours of the Rooster
7 p.m. to	9 p.m.	The hours of the Dog
9 p.m. to	11 p.m.	The hours of the Pig

Rat: The influence of the Rat as ascendant is likely to make the sign more outgoing, sociable and also more careful with money. A particularly beneficial influence for those born under the sign of the Rabbit, Horse, Monkey and Pig.

Ox: The Ox as ascendant has a restraining, cautionary and steadying influence which many signs will benefit from. This ascendant also promotes self-confidence and will-power and is an especially good ascendant for those born under the signs of the Tiger, Rabbit and Goat.

Tiger: This ascendant is a dynamic and stirring influence which makes the sign more outgoing, more action-orientated and more impulsive. A generally favourable ascendant for the Ox, Tiger, Snake and Horse.

Rabbit: The Rabbit as ascendant has a moderating influence, making the sign more reflective, serene and discreet. A particularly beneficial influence for the Rat, Dragon, Monkey and Rooster.

Dragon: The Dragon as ascendant gives strength, determination and an added ambition to the sign. A favourable influence for those born under the signs of the Rabbit, Goat, Monkey and Dog.

Snake: The Snake as ascendant can make the sign more reflective, more intuitive and more self-reliant. A good influence for the Tiger, Goat and Pig.

Horse: The influence of the Horse will make the sign more adventurous, more daring and, on some occasions, more fickle. Generally a beneficial influence for the Rabbit, Snake, Dog and Pig.

Goat: This ascendant will make the sign more tolerant, easy-going and receptive. The Goat could also impart some creative and artistic qualities to the sign. An especially good influence for the Ox, Dragon, Snake and Rooster.

Monkey: The Monkey as ascendant is likely to impart a delicious sense of humour and fun to the sign. He will make the sign more enterprising and outgoing – a particularly good influence for the Rat, Ox, Snake and Goat.

Rooster: The Rooster as ascendant helps to give the sign a lively, outgoing and very methodical manner. Its influence will increase efficiency and is a good influence for the Ox, Tiger, Rabbit and Horse.

Dog: The Dog as ascendant makes the sign more reasonable and fair-minded as well as giving an added sense of loyalty. A very good ascendant for the Tiger, Dragon and Goat.

Pig: The influence of the Pig can make the sign more sociable, content and self-indulgent. It is also a caring influence and one which can make the sign want to help others. A good ascendant for the Dragon and Monkey.

How to Get the Best from the Year

One of the chief values of Chinese horoscopes is that they help to identify trends for the forthcoming year. Once these trends have been identified, it is possible for each sign to know what areas of life are likely to proceed well and which could prove more troublesome. With this knowledge, the more favourably aspected areas can be concentrated on and care can be taken in those areas where the aspects are not so favourable. In this respect, Chinese horoscopes can serve as a useful guide.

Here, to supplement the earlier sections on the prospects

for each of the signs, I have indicated how I believe each of the signs will fare in 1993 and how each can get the best from the year. The areas covered are: general prospects, finance, career prospects and relations with others.

General Prospects

Rat: A busy and fulfilling year. Great progress can be made, but to maximize the favourable trends the Rat should be methodical and organized. He would do well to set himself some priorities for the year and avoid starting projects he cannot deal with properly or has no time to complete. Efficient use of time will bring its rewards. Travel prospects are good.

Ox: A most satisfying year ahead. The Ox will benefit from the Rooster's desire for method and order, and by planning his activities carefully, he can make great progress. He should, however, be prepared to involve others in his plans and set about his various activities in his usual determined manner.

Tiger: This will be a positive and constructive year for the Tiger. He would do well to have some idea of his priorities and objectives for the year and avoid the temptation of committing himself to too many activities at any one time. He should also try to curb his sometimes rebellious and forthright tendencies – to make good progress over the year, he needs the support of others and to inflame the feelings of those around him unnecessarily could easily rebound on him. This is a year for diplomacy and dedication to his objectives! Travel is well aspected.

Rabbit: This will not be the easiest of years for the Rabbit. However, providing he is prepared to be patient and persevering, he can turn what could be an indifferent year into a most useful one. This is a year for watching, listening and planning. The experience the Rabbit gains, the plans he makes and any additional skills he can gain will prove very useful to him in the future.

Dragon: A highly favourable year. A year for action, for the Dragon to pursue his aims and ambitions in his own determined style. With a positive outlook, much can be achieved.

Snake: An excellent and rewarding year ahead. The Snake should go after his objectives in a positive and determined manner. With the right attitude, his progress and achievements over the year can be truly considerable.

Horse: A reasonably good year when hard work and a persistent attitude will bring rewards. Travel will prove particularly enjoyable.

Goat: A promising and fulfilling year ahead. If the Goat is in any way dissatisfied with his present position, this is the year for him to remedy the situation! Throughout the year he should act positively and be determined to make the best of his many abilities. Much can be accomplished in 1993 and the changes and events that take place are likely to be to the Goat's long-term advantage.

Monkey: This will be a generally pleasant although reasonably busy year for the Monkey. He should try to spread his activities out over the year and avoid taking on too many commitments at any one time. Not all the events will go in his favour and he could experience some set-backs, but by being adaptable and resourceful, the Monkey will be able to overcome any difficulties that arise and emerge from the year with many gains to his credit. Travel is very well aspected.

Rooster: A successful and fulfilling year. Many opportunities await the Rooster in this, his own year, and he should pursue his aims and objectives in his usual meticulous and positive way. Much can be achieved.

Dog: A challenging year ahead, but provided the Dog sets about his various activities in his usual careful and conscientious manner he will sow the seeds of his future success. This is a year of preparation and steady progress; 1994 will be the year when the Dog will reap the real rewards of his work and efforts.

Pig: The Pig will see a considerable improvement taking place this year. Those around him will be more amenable towards his ideas and plans, and progress is possible in many of his activities. Throughout the year the Pig should act positively and go after his objectives in a resolute manner. If he has experienced setbacks in recent years, he should remember that many Pigs have achieved great things after triumphing over difficulties and obstacles and 1993 can, with the right attitude, be a successful and fulfilling year for him.

Finance

Rat: The Rat should be careful in money matters over the year and particularly watch his level of outgoings.

Ox: This is a year for prudence and the Ox would be wise to keep a close watch on his expenditure and not commit himself to any major venture without checking the facts beforehand. As far as possible, he should avoid lending to others.

Tiger: Although the Tiger could incur some large expenses in 1993, financial matters will generally go well.

Rabbit: Fortunately the Rabbit is most astute in financial matters, for 1993 is very much a year for care and prudence. The Rabbit should be careful in any large transaction that he enters into and should make sure that he understands all the implications of any new agreement. This is not a year for speculation or gambling.

Dragon: Financial matters will go well, although the Dragon would be wise not to squander any spare funds that he might have. Any spare money could be usefully spent on home improvements or travel (which is well aspected) or put into a savings policy which would make provision for the future.

Snake: The Snake will do well in financial matters in 1993 provided he steers clear of speculative and risky enterprises.

Horse: The Horse will be fortunate in financial matters over the year and can look forward to a general improvement in his financial situation.

Goat: Although this will be an enjoyable year for the Goat, it could also prove an expensive one. Throughout 1993 the Goat would do well to keep a close watch on his outgoings and it would be in his interest to exercise a certain amount of restraint in his spending.

Monkey: Financial matters will go well providing the Monkey does not take risks or enter into speculative ventures. The Monkey should be particularly wary of any dubious schemes or offers that he may come across. All is not what it seems.

Rooster: A generally favourable year for financial matters. However, the Rooster would do well to keep tabs on his general level of outgoings and also closely examine the costs involved in any major purchase that he is about to make.

Dog: This year the Dog should be careful and prudent in financial matters. He should avoid taking risks and lending to others and would do well to watch his general level of expenditure.

Pig: The Pig can look forward to an improvement in his financial situation. However, he does need to keep a close watch over his level of expenditure. Any savings he can make will prove most useful, particularly in the latter part of the year when he may want to take a holiday, buy something for his house or make an expensive purchase.

Career Prospects

Rat: A good time work-wise. The Rat should go after any opportunities he sees. If he gets the chance to widen his skills and experience, he will find that this will prove of great value and will do much to enhance his prospects.

Ox: The Ox can make considerable progress in work matters and this could prove an opportune year for seeking a new position or taking up a new type of work.

Tiger: The Tiger will make useful and positive progress in his work over the year. He should advance his ideas and go after the opportunities he sees.

Rabbit: Although the Rabbit can expect to make modest progress, he cannot afford to take risks. In all his business activities he needs to proceed with care and make sure that he has the support of others. In case of problems, he should be discreet and patient. For those seeking work, there will be opportunities to pursue and anything the Rabbit can do to further his skills and gain qualifications will prove very helpful in the future.

Dragon: Great progress can be made this year. New opportunities, improved prospects, promotion and a new job are all possible and the Dragon should act with fortitude and go after the opportunities that will present themselves.

Snake: Work matters are very favourably aspected. The Snake should promote himself and his talents to the best of his abilities. A new job or promotion is certainly possible.

Horse: The Horse will do well in his work. However, to get the best results, he will need to work hard and concentrate on specific objectives.

Goat: The Goat can make significant progress over the year. If he is dissatisfied with his present situation or is seeking promotion or a new job, he should follow up any new opportunities and openings he sees. This is a good year for him to seize the initiative and make the most of his many skills and abilities. With resolution and determination, the Goat's progress and achievements can be great indeed!

Monkey: The Monkey can look forward to making good and steady progress in his career. Throughout the year he should remain alert for new opportunities to pursue and if he is able to add to his skills, he will find this will do much to improve his prospects.

Rooster: Great progress is possible. However, the Rooster will need to work hard in order to secure the results he desires. By remaining diligent and vigilant, he can do extremely well in his career.

Dog: The Dog should proceed slowly and carefully. Progress can be made, but he should avoid taking risks. Any additional skills or qualifications he can obtain will prove of great value in the future.

Pig: A year of constructive and positive progress. The Pig should continue to set about his own activities in his usual methodical and conscientious manner, but at the same time seek out opportunities to pursue and, if possible, find ways in which he can add to his skills. With determination and persistence, he can do extremely well.

Relations with Others

Rat: A generally happy year, with favourable prospects for making new friends. Romance and marriage are very well aspected.

Ox: This will be a very happy and sociable year. Those around the Ox will be most supportive and co-operative. The Ox will make several valuable friends and acquaintances over the year and it is also a good year for romance!

Tiger: A happy and contented year socially and domestically. However, the Tiger should make every effort to involve others in his activities. The spring and summer months are likely to be a particularly enjoyable time.

Rabbit: Although in other areas, the year may not proceed as well as the Rabbit may wish, he can take comfort from the knowledge that his relations with others are well aspected

Those around him will be ready to help and support him and, if he does have any matters that are troubling him, he should not hesitate to seek the opinion of others. Domestically and socially, 1993 will be a good and generally happy year.

Dragon: Domestically, a good year. The Dragon will find those around him helpful and co-operative. A good year for making new friends but for romance to truly blossom, the Dragon should let new relationships develop naturally rather than rush into any commitment. Generally though, a happy year.

Snake: A pleasant and enjoyable year. The Snake's family and friends will be most supportive. There are, however, many Snakes who tend to be 'loners' and keep themselves to themselves. In 1993 these Snakes should make every effort to overcome their reserved nature by going out more and meeting others. If they can do this, 1993 will be one of the most enjoyable years they have had for a long time.

Horse: A good year socially and domestically. However, the Horse does need to handle his relations with others with care over the year. He cannot afford to ignore others' views and should make every effort to involve those around him in his various activities. An independent and 'go-it-alone' attitude will only hamper his progress and possibly sour his relations with others. Provided he bears this in mind, the Horse will find this a most pleasant year.

Goat: Domestically and socially, this will be a good year. However, the Goat should make every effort to be more open in expressing his views and feelings. To keep his thoughts and feelings to himself could impair his relations with others and result in friction and misunderstandings.

Monkey: A busy year socially and domestically. However, the Monkey would do well to ensure that he devotes time to his family and friends and does not get so wrapped up in his own concerns that he ignores the interests of others. If he remembers this, he can look forward to some splendid and enjoyable times. If not, domestic tensions will arise and the Monkey's relations with others could suffer. With care and forethought, however, this can be avoided.

Rooster: Domestically, a happy and settled year. The Rooster does, however, need to ensure that he involves others in his activities and has the necessary support and backing for any new project he may undertake. Those around him will be generally co-operative and supportive, but the Rooster cannot take their support for granted!

Dog: Throughout the year the Dog should pay careful attention to the views of those around him and avoid becoming too preoccupied with his own activities. He should try to be more open in expressing his feelings and views. The Dog should also remember that there are many who hold him in great affection and who are willing to help him if he needs assistance or a second opinion. He will also make some very good friends over the year.

Pig: The sociable Pig will be on top form this year and will enjoy a good social life and a generally content and happy domestic life. Any Pigs who may have recently felt lonely or faced personal problems will find that a noticeable improvement will take place during 1993. This is a year for the Pig to enjoy himself. If he finds he has too much to contend with, however, he should not hesitate to ask for support.

Also available . . .

Your Personal Horoscope 1993

Month-by-month forecasts for every sign

Joseph Polansky

Whatever your sign, *Your Personal Horoscope 1993* shows you how to make the most of your life in the coming year by taking full advantage of the planetary influences. Sign by sign, the book includes:

- Yearly forecasts highlighting celestial trends for love and romance, home and the family, career and money.

- Month-by-month forecasts pinpointing your best and worst days.

- Penetrating character analyses – how each zodiac sign behaves with money, at work and in love.

- Powerful insights into the lifestyles of each sign – their domestic and social life, health and relationships.

Understanding your own sign and the astrological influences for 1993 will help you bring out the best in yourself and the year to come. *Your Personal Horoscope 1993* is the next best thing to having your own personal astrologer!

Understanding Astrology

First steps in chart interpretation

Sasha Fenton

Understanding Astrology provides a concise introduction to the ancient art of astrology, showing how it can be used to assess a person's character. Ingenious short-cuts and quick-clue summaries are given to help the beginner quickly grasp the basic ideas, and all aspects of astrology are covered, from elements, houses and hemispheres to planets and their influence. ·

Complete with diagrams, sample birth charts and a glossary of terms, this book serves as an ideal starting point for anyone taking their first steps in the fascinating study of astrology.

Power Astrology

Make the most of your sun sign

Robin MacNaughton

The degree of satisfaction with which you experience every moment of life fully is measured by the extent of your personal power over your life.

With a depth of insight previously unwitnessed in any astrology book, Robin McNaughton explains clearly and concisely her conclusions to achieving that special control over your life. Through daily mental exercises – specially designed for each of the twelve signs – she reveals how to achieve true mastery over your life in order to enrich your experiences. *Power Astrology* shows how to overcome emotional stumbling blocks, increase positive spirit and energize your mind.

What Number Are You?

Your numbers and your life

Lilla Bek & Robert Holden

Your birthdate, your birthplace and your name each have their own individual numbers. So too has each year, each month and each day of your life. *What Number Are You?* translates the language of numbers. It helps you to identify the essential numbers in your life and tells you exactly what these numbers may mean to you.

The study of numbers is an exciting exploration and adventure into an ancient tradition of personal development and self-realization. The ultimate aim of numerology is to fit in, to synchronise and to make peace – with both the world around us and the world within us. This is numerology.

The Chinese Astrology Workbook

How to calculate and interpret Chinese horoscopes

Derek Walters

There is far more to Chinese astrology than the personality types of Rat, Tiger, Monkey, etc. Traditional Chinese astrology is used, in fact, far more for divinatory purposes than for character analysis, and this practical guide therefore follows this bias.

With the aid of a glossary and numerous worksheets and charts, *The Chinese Astrology Workbook* takes the student into the fascinating world of Chinese astrology: the intricacies of the Chinese calendar; both planetary and Purple Crepe Myrtle astrology (that based on the stars of the Great Bear); the Five Elements, vital to Chinese philosophy as well as their astrology; the Chinese interpretation of the five planets and its fundamental differences from the Western view; constructing and interpreting the final horoscope – all are explained clearly and methodically so that even the complete novice can grasp easily the concepts of Chinese astrology.

YOUR PERSONAL HOROSCOPE
1993   1 85538 173 7   £5.99 ☐
UNDERSTANDING ASTROLOGY   1 85538 065 X   £4.99 ☐
POWER ASTROLOGY   1 85538 160 5   £4.99 ☐
WHAT NUMBER ARE YOU?   1 85538 135 4   £5.99 ☐
WHAT COLOUR ARE YOU?   0 85030 616 7   £4.99 ☐
THE CHINESE ASTROLOGY
WORKBOOK   0 85030 641 8   £6.99 ☐

All these books are available from your local bookseller or can
be ordered direct from the publishers.

To order direct just tick the titles you want and fill in the form
below:

Name: _____

Address:_____

_____

_____ Postcode:_____

Send to: Thorsons Mail Order, Dept 3Y, HarperCollins*Publishers*,
Westerhill Road, Bishopbriggs, Glasgow G64 2QT.
Please enclose a cheque or postal order to debit my Visa/Access
account –

Credit card no: _____

Expiry date: _____

Signature: _____

– to the value of the cover price plus:
UK & BFPO: Add £1.00 for the first book and 25p for each
additional book ordered.
Overseas orders including Eire: Please add £2.95 service
charge. Books will be sent by surface mail but quotes for airmail
despatches will be given on request.

24 HOUR TELEPHONE ORDERING SERVICE FOR ACCESS/
VISA CARDHOLDERS – TEL: **041 772 2281.**